interiorscapes

interiorscapes

GARDENS WITHIN BUILDINGS

PAUL COOPER

MITCHELL BEAZLEY

INTERIORSCAPES
Paul Cooper

First published in 2003
by Mitchell Beazley,
an imprint of Octopus Publishing Group Ltd,
2–4 Heron Quays, London E14 4JP

ISBN 1 84000 607 2

A CIP catalogue copy of this book is available
from the British Library

Executive Art Director **Christie Cooper**
Commissioning Editor **Michèle Byam**
Design **Amzie Viladot**
Contributing Editor **Richard Dawes**
Production Controller **Kieran Connelly**
Picture Researcher **Sarah Hopper**
Indexer **Sue Farr**

Set in Bembo

Printed and bound in China by
Toppan Printing Company Limited

Half title page: Sound Garden, Parc de la Villette, Paris;
designed by Bernard Leitner; photo Pascal Dolémieux.
Opposite title page: The Hawkinson Garden, Arizona;
designed by Steve Martino; photo Charles Mann
Photography Inc.
Right: Washington State Convention and Trade Center,
Seattle; Danadjieva & Koenig Associates; photo J.F. Housel.

contents ▶ ▶ ▶ ▶ ▶

This book is not about simply decorating the house or workplace with plants. It is a survey of designed, architecture-related, contemporary gardens and landscapes in both private and public spaces. An "interiorscape" is a garden that is a part of a building's architecture, whereas a garden or landscape more often surrounds a building. Interiorscapes include gardens that are within buildings, either covered or open to the air, as well as gardens that, although not contained by the architecture, are intrinsic to it. They are all gardens that have an intimate link with an architectural structure, sometimes depending on it physically or as a means of defining boundaries and even their function. They can be gardens designed as extensions of buildings, and they include some roof gardens as well as gardens that have more unorthodox relationships with the concerned building.

In the West the idea of the garden is inseparable from plants, but in this book it is regarded as a much broader concept. Like the Japanese raked-gravel gardens, it may or may not include plants. Many interiorscapes are created by landscape architects and are referred to as "landscapes" even though they often do not involve a transformation of the land or ground but utilize an architectural structure.

The garden designed as an integral part of a building is becoming increasingly commonplace, but it is by no means a recent development in garden history. It is, however, often neglected, since the more visible evolution of the garden has been the development of man-made landscapes around, in front of, or behind properties. For over the centuries garden designers have aimed to extend the garden outwards and away from the building. Prime examples are the gardens created in the "grand manner" in the seventeenth century, such as those at Versaille in France. Here, formal vistas were used to give the illusion of the grounds extending endlessly. In England in the eighteenth century a new style lead by William Kent and Lancelot "Capability" Brown favoured a more informal, natural-looking garden. Here, devices such as the ha-ha were used to conceal boundary lines and link the garden with the landscape beyond.

However, the history of garden design also includes gardens that were both more modest in scale and less obvious because they were confined and concealed within buildings. As far back as the fifth century BC in Greece, private houses contained paved internal courtyards, surrounded by colonnades, in which plants were grown in pots and tubs. By the

◀ One of the main reasons why gardens were created within buildings was as a response to the climate. In fourteenth-century Timbuktu (in what is now Mali) gardens were not only contained within architectural walls but also sunken to protect them from the winds. In addition they were more easily irrigated because they were nearer the water table.

The garden of the Casa de Vettii at Pompeii, Italy, was buried in the eruption of Vesuvius in AD 79 but comparatively recently rediscovered and restored. It is one of the few surviving examples of the peristyle garden of ancient Rome. Contained within the villa, this courtyard is an open-air ornamental garden surrounded by a portico that has walls decorated with murals.

fourth century Alexander the Great had conquered Persia and Egypt, where planted flower gardens were already popular. In the new and expanding Hellenistic world, the Greek courtyards became dedicated to the growing of exotic plants and flowers.

In the third century BC Hellenistic style became Roman style. This affected the design of the Roman villa, the layout of which was modified to enclose a private garden. Building and garden were designed as one, with the garden space formed of a courtyard surrounded by a covered walkway supported by a colonnade. This was clearly an adaptation of the courtyard found in earlier Greek houses. Often referred to as a "peristyle" garden, it contained shrubs and flowers as well as ornamental pools and fountains. The covered walkway provided shade, while the open-air central area helped to ventilate the adjoining rooms.

When the Roman Empire fell to the Barbarians, villas fell into ruins and devoted followers of the new faith of Christianity sought refuge in isolated, close-knit communities. The early Benedictine monasteries, dating from the end of the fifth century, contained enclosed central areas called cloisters. They resembled Roman courtyards, with roofed pillared walks on all four sides. They were used for meditation and, to make the space more conducive to this, ornamental gardens were often included at the centre.

In Japan, the design of the traditional garden seeks to give visual expression to religious ideas, derived originally from Shinto and later from Zen Buddhism. Inspired by the philosophy that all living things have their own spirit, the creators of the earliest Japanese gardens were concerned not with imitating nature but with capturing its spirit by the use of symbols. The ultimate realization of these symbolic landscapes became the waterless and plantless Zen gardens or "dry landscapes." In traditional dwellings small dry landscapes consisting of raked gravel and stones were

▲ The courtyard garden
known as the Patio de la
Riadh was constructed
in the fourteenth century
within the walls of
the Generalife, near the
Alhambra, in Granada,
Spain. What are perhaps
the most attractive features
of the courtyard are both
based on the use of water,
a characteristic of Moorish
architecture. narrow
canal runs the entire
length of the walled
garden and numerous
fountains keep the space
pleasantly cool in the
hot summer months.

often integrated within the house, a tradition that continues in Kyoto today.

From the nineteenth century, more secular courtyard gardens appeared in Japanese towns. These gardens correspond to the arrangement often found in the West in which a shopkeeper or tradesman carries on his business at the front of a premises while living at the back. In Japan such an arrangement included gardens and was based on a standard plan. A passage led from the shop at the front into a first garden and then across to the main living quarters. Here, another corridor, beside which is a second garden, led to the rear of the house. This, in turn, was separated from a storage area at the back by another garden space. Some of these multi-courtyard gardens still exist.

While in the sixth century Buddhism was expanding from China into Japan, the Arabs were taking Islam east into Persia and across North Africa into Spain. A dependence on water was a central feature of the ancient Persian gardens and this continued to be reflected in the design of Islamic gardens. The Islamic residential gardens of the seventh and eighth centuries were mainly courtyards; they suited the climate, with welcome shade provided by the architecture. These courtyard gardens were usually rectangular, with central pavilions placed at the intersection of four water channels. Planting was confined to clearly defined borders situated towards the perimeter of the space. The Arabs took the knowledge of building gardens that they had acquired from Persia into the other countries they conquered, most notably, Spain.

The architecture and enclosed gardens associated with Moorish Spain first appeared in the eighth century. It is, however, the Alhambra in Granada, dating from the thirteenth century, where the Moorish atmosphere can be best appreciated, since it is here that the gardens are so closely integrated with the buildings that they are architecturally as one. Although the palace has changed over the years, four garden courts remain. The Court of the Lions, with its elaborate colonnade, is divided into four by shallow irrigation channels, as in traditional Persian gardens. The Court of the Myrtles features a central long, rectangular pond bordered by paths and more recently planted myrtles.

Above the Alhambra is the Generalife. Situated on a hillside and created in the fourteenth century, it also contains Moorish courtyard gardens, including the "Patio de la Riadh," which features a narrow canal that runs, unusually, the whole length of the planted courtyard or patio. "Patio" is the Spanish word for an inner courtyard.

Although Léon Battista Alberti, in his treatise of 1492, spelled out the need for the Renaissance house and garden to be integrated, he also suggested that it should be wedded to the landscape. What followed was a garden that looked outwards, not inwards, with terraces giving spectacular views. Alberti's philosophy was to influence the design of gardens for great villas, houses, and palaces for centuries.

An obsession with flowers, collected and imported, was to stimulate the next development in the history of gardens within buildings. Many of the importers of these plants were from Northern European countries with colonies in warmer lands. Not all the imported plants were hardy enough to

▲ The nineteenth-century enthusiasm for collecting plants called for large greenhouses. This one, at Tatton Park, Cheshire, England, is made from cast iron rather than the wood widely used earlier and was built to house a collection of ferns.

◀ The Crystal Palace, built in London for the Great Exhibition of 1851, was designed as a temporary structure with reusable parts that could be dismantled easily. It was given a large barrel vault to accommodate a number of existing large elms. Adorned with fountains, sculptures, and exotic planting, this was one of the first indoor winter gardens.

withstand the harsh northern winters and they had to be protected. Great glasshouses were erected to contain the botanical collections brought home by the nineteenth-century plant hunters. The Palm House at Kew, London, was built for this purpose. At the same time conservatories, or winter gardens, as they were sometimes called, were being built to provide wealthier members of society with all-year pleasure gardens. These structures were made possible as a result of the industrial revolution, with the use of frameworks made of iron instead of wood coinciding with improvements in glass manufacture.

The increase in gardens and landscapes created within or on buildings during the last century can be attributed to many factors. Further advances in the design and construction of buildings have contributed to the creation of new types of enclosed spaces and to the lessening of the distinction

▲ In the Japanese city of Kyoto traditional architecture is still in evidence. This is the entrance to a restaurant with the "entrance garden" behind it. In the traditional Japanese house the entrance garden was a place in which to greet guests and here it welcomes diners. This feature indicates how the garden is regarded as an integral part of both culture and architecture.

► This interior view of an inn built in the traditional style in Kyoto shows a small garden enclosed within a *sodegaki*, or bamboo screen. The traditional Japanese garden and house were conceived as one, with the principal interior spaces designed to open directly on to an exterior, enclosed garden.

between interior and exterior space. New functions for this new architecture, such as corporate headquarters and shopping malls, have provided new opportunities for interior gardens. More recently, a growing awareness of ecological issues has encouraged an increase in planting within buildings and in the urban environment. Urban congestion remains a problem and has forced gardens into buildings and, in some cases, on to the tops of them.

While this book does not cover the roof garden in depth, it is important in the development of the relationship between garden and architecture. There were roof gardens in Roman times, such as that at the Villa Diomedes in Pompeii; this villa had a terrace strong enough to support an extensive area of planting. Roof gardens also played a part in the integration of house and garden that occurred in the Renaissance, and *c.*1400 Cosimo de' Medici built a roof garden on his villa near Florence. However, their development was slow until the nineteenth century, when in 1867 Carl Rabbitz, a master builder, exhibited in Paris a plaster model of a roof garden that he had built on his house in Berlin. What stimulated most interest was that the flat roof and its garden were on top of an ordinary house in northern Europe rather than a warm and dry region.

In the twentieth century, new building methods using steel and concrete led to further developments by providing increasingly strong flat-roof structures promoted as helping to beautify cities, gaining leisure space, and providing gardens in congested cities.

The motivation behind the creation of modern roof gardens is also one of the principal reasons for making gardens within buildings. When competition for space on the ground is great, gardens are unable to have their own exclusive space and need to share it with the architecture. Planting can improve air quality in cities and towns as well as being a natural sound absorber, and these environmental benefits have prompted an interest in a "greener" architecture.

Interiorscapes serve many purposes. They can provide a refuge from the pace and pressure of daily life or create all-weather social environments, but whatever their function, in all cases the gardens are in the buildings rather than the buildings in the gardens.

▲ The M House, in Tokyo, designed by Kazuyo Sejima and Ryue Nishizawa, contains a sunken courtyard garden with a single specimen of flowering dogwood (*Cornus florida*) growing at one end. Together, this house and garden represent a continuation of the ancient Japanese tradition of integration of the two elements. At the same time this minimal garden has more in common with twentieth-century modernism than it does with the traditional Zen Buddhist garden.

inner sanctuaries ▶

"HEAVEN," SOGETSU SCHOOL OF FLOWER ARRANGEMENT, TOKYO, JAPAN

LANDSCAPE DESIGNER: **ISAMU NOGUCHI**

▲ In the entrance hall, in a work that continues the Japanese Zen garden tradition, Noguchi used sparsely carved blocks of granite to create an abstract interpretation of a mountain landscape.

▶ Noguchi has included the simplest of water features in his "mountain" landscape. Water emerges from a cup-shaped stone and flows via precisely cut, shallow channels through a circular pool to a waterfall. Here it gently pours down into another circular pool cut into a stone cube that is out of view.

A sanctuary is usually defined as a place of refuge, and historically this would have been a holy place or sacred building where a fugitive could seek safety. Today the word is also used to describe a peaceful place, conducive to contemplation and providing escape from the rigours of the modern world. Gardens have long been seen as serving this purpose, and when a garden lies within the confines of a building the sense of sanctuary is reinforced.

The enclosed garden as a sanctuary has been an essential part of Japanese architecture and culture for centuries. In Kyoto, in central Japan, the tradition continues today, and one finds traditional houses built as recently as the 1990s that have the familiar membrane walls and dry garden. The inclusion of a small, sunken garden of raked gravel with standing stones, surrounded by a wooden walkway, continues the Japanese architectural concept of "inside outside." The organization of the traditional Japanese house emphasized the relationship between these two domains. The garden is part of the interior, and the living space is part of the exterior. In this tradition of garden-making, walls are delicate, transparent divisions that allow a sense of flow between the inside and outside realms, and this emphasis on freedom of movement is essential to Zen theology. The external landscape is brought "inside," into the garden, by an interpretation of its features in a miniature form, using stone "islands" or

Horai stones. This interior garden, drawing on the Zen idea of "borrowing scenery," was intended as a symbolic representation of the paradise that is nature.

This idea of creating a symbolic equivalent of the landscape was developed by the Japanese-American sculptor Isamu Noguchi in his design for an interior feature for the Sogetsu School of Flower Arrangement in Tokyo. Noguchi's solution is less traditional and formulaic but nonetheless involves a landscape brought inside. The work, "Heaven," executed in the mid-1970s, is like a giant *tokonoma* – a place in a Japanese house reserved for flower arrangements and seen as the most sacred, and therefore most "heavenly," part of the home.

Noguchi was born in 1904 in Los Angeles, but spent his formative years at school in Japan. He became interested in Japanese prehistoric art and the traditional stone-and-raked gravel Zen garden, so it is not surprising that he began to develop sculptural ideas that could be expressed in terms of landscapes.

He realized his ambition to create sculptural landscapes in the mid-1950s when he completed a garden at the UNESCO headquarters in Paris, and by the middle of the 1960s he had created two sunken, enclosed gardens. The first was for the Beinecke Rare Book and Manuscript Library at Yale University, Connecticut, the second was for the Chase Manhattan Bank in New York. The garden at Yale consists of three geometric, white marble forms;

one is based on a cube, another on a pyramid, and a third on a circle. These forms are arranged on a stone floor inscribed with a grid pattern. A sort of modernist Zen garden, it is the most minimalist of Noguchi's contained "gardens." The sunken circular garden in the plaza of the Chase Manhattan Bank is more closely based on the traditional Japanese Zen garden and the "borrowed" or miniature landscape, with eroded black river boulders carefully placed in the garden's fountain pool to suggest islands.

In the mid-1970s Noguchi began building his indoor granite "mountain landscape" for the Sogetsu School. The "mountain" as a sculptural form is a recurring motif in his work and appears in his sculpture and theatre designs and his environmental projects. The Sogetsu School's building was designed by the Japanese architect Kenzo Tange and had in its lobby a stepped structure forming part of an indoor roof of a theatre that was on a lower level. Noguchi was asked to give purpose to this architectural anomaly. Without altering the structure's architectural integrity, he has transformed Tange's ledges into the abstract "mountain," complete with ridges, geometric ledges, overhangs, and cascading water. Constructed from large blocks of economically carved stone, it acts as a display area for the school's flower arrangers. In some places the stone is highly finished or polished; elsewhere it is left in a rough, unfinished-looking state. In the cave-like cavity near the steps the rough stone adds textural interest and a sense of mystery to this shaded void. The cut flowers provide the only "planting" in this dry garden.

A respect for Japan's culture is also evident in Akihiko Takeuchi's design for the Centre for Japanese Studies at the University of Indonesia, in West Java.

CENTRE FOR JAPANESE STUDIES, UNIVERSITY OF INDONESIA, WEST JAVA
ARCHITECT: **AKIHIKO TAKEUCHI**

▶ Takeuchi's Japanese-style courtyard garden uses stones and a grassy mound to depict the main islands in the Indonesian archipelago.

CANADIAN EMBASSY, TOKYO, JAPAN

LANDSCAPE ARCHITECT: **SHUNMYO MASUNO**

▲ A view from above of the stone-and-gravel garden in the basement shows how Masuno uses gravels of different colours to highlight the segments defined by lines of stones.

▶ Masuno's preliminary drawing for the basement shows a reworking of the traditional Japanese Zen garden of stone and gravel. This plantless garden, a practical solution for a basement, provides interest in what would otherwise have been an uninviting area.

In this building, completed in 1995, Takeuchi followed traditional Japanese architectural practice by arranging the group of buildings that comprise the campus in an informal manner around a central seminar building. This, in turn, encloses an internal courtyard space that has a traditional garden of stone and gravel. The garden is a modern interpretation of the ancient *karesansui*, or "dry landscape," garden.

Living nature is reorganized, abstracted, and condensed in the *karesansui*, which was seen as a way of communicating the concepts of Zen Buddhism. In keeping with a philosophy of non-literal and idealistic religious expression, these gardens, which originated in the mid-fifteenth century, consisted mainly of carefully placed rocks and raked gravel with a few well-chosen plants. In later gardens plants were replaced by small clusters of moss. Large boulders were used to evoke waterfalls and horizontal slabs represented bridges. Many *karesansui* temple gardens were very small, often contained within buildings, and were to be viewed from roofed passageways, usually located along one side.

The design of the *karesansui* at the Centre for Japanese Studies also recalls the peristyle courtyard gardens associated with Roman villas, with a terracotta-tiled roof passage that allows the garden to

**HOUSEHOLD FINANCE
CORPORATION BUILDING,
CHICAGO, USA**

ARCHITECTS: **LOEBL,
SCHLOSSMAN & HACKL**

▶ Subtropical vegetation,
including tree ferns and
palms, fills the atrium.
Rough-textured stone walls,
irregularly shaped pools,
and waterfalls recall
the naturalistic style of
landscaping that was
popular in the 1970s.

▼ The forceful naturalism
of this garden achieves
an effective contrast
with the luxurious glass
and gilt detailing of the
atrium surrounding it.

be viewed from all sides rather than just one. A modern addition is the introduction, between the roof-supporting uprights, of glass panels to protect the onlooker from tropical rainstorms. The garden itself consists of rounded boulders and mounds of turf, placed to mimic the islands of Indonesia.

Shunmyo Masuno's design for the landscaping within the Canadian Embassy in Tokyo also continues the tradition of the Japanese Zen garden. He is well qualified to interpret and develop this tradition, for he studied landscape architecture in Tokyo and then, in 1979, entered the Daihonzan-Soji-ji temple, where he underwent ascetic training to become a priest. By 1985 Masuno had both established a landscape-design consultancy and become an assistant priest at the Kenkoh-ji temple in Yokohama.

The main gardens of the Embassy are laid out in exterior spaces within the structure of the building. Some are under cover and are located to the front of the fourth-floor reception area, and their purpose is symbolic rather than recreational. The brief required that the landscape design should symbolize and reinforce the relationship between Canada and Japan, with their very different cultures. In response Masuno planned and created two distinct gardens.

The Canada Garden is intended to express a sense of scenic grandeur, while the Japanese garden was designed to convey a sense of "joy in detail and delicacy." Masuno's commission also called for the creation of a landscape feature in front of the Cityclub of Tokyo facility in the basement of the Embassy. The stone-and-gravel garden, which can also be viewed from the floors above, is a further modern interpretation of the historic Japanese Zen garden. Contained within walls, these gardens of stone-and-raked gravel are not to be entered or walked upon but are to be considered as aids to contemplation, like a "sermon in stones."

The basement garden's raked gravel and carefully chosen and positioned stones belong to the ancient tradition, but the overall design is inspired by geometry and mathematics rather than the natural landscape of Japan. It is based on a logarithmic spiral, the distinctive features of which are that it does not change its shape as it expands and it has no beginning

▲ A bronze sculpture provides a discreet focal point within the exotic interior landscape of the atrium. Pathways lead from the offices into the garden, where staff and visitors can relax by walking amid lush greenery, soothed by the sound of a waterfall.

and no end, progressing outward and inward to infinity. Masuno uses this geometric model to express what he describes as "the idea of spouting energy." At the same time this "garden" provides a place of contemplation, a peaceful sanctuary in what is otherwise a busy, convivial, and lively part of the Embassy, where Masuno completed his work in 1991.

In addition to providing a place of retreat from the pressures of life, a sanctuary can also be regarded as answering more basic needs. In the USA and Canada, where temperatures vary between -20°C (-4°F) and 35°C (95°F), the term might be applied to

a place of refuge from climatic extremes. In the early 1960s a few architects realized that the creation of a large, interior, temperature-controlled, and planted environment within a building could provide a sanctuary, or at least temporary respite, from cold weather in particular. The indoor atrium built in 1978 as part of the Household Finance Corporation Building in Chicago, the "Windy City," is a place where one can walk and take exercise in comparative comfort. What makes using this space so pleasurable is the inclusion of a tropical-style garden, complete with waterfalls and a pool. It remains a luxurious

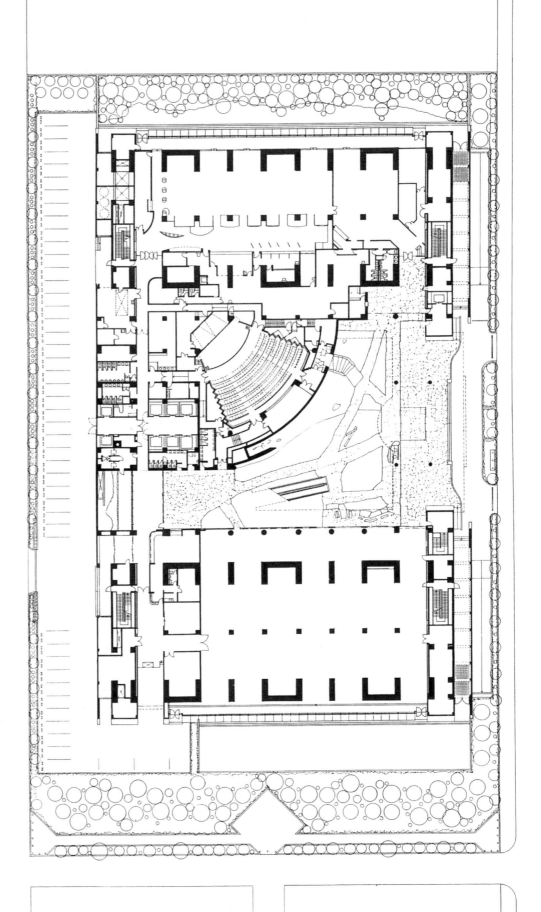

▶ The architect's drawing of the ground floor of the Matsushita Building shows that the stone paths are an important feature of the central atrium. These lead to elevators and the offices on either side of the open space, as well as passing across an expanse of water to give access to the lecture theatre.

**THE SHUTTERS HOUSE,
LOS ANGELES,
CALIFORNIA, USA**
ARCHITECTS: **MOORE RUBLE
& YUDELL**

◄ In a recess in the far wall of the courtyard garden is a water-ladder down which water tumbles into a shallow pool that occupies the whole floor space. Rough-cut flagstones add textural interest to the pool and their unevenness is also intended to deter entry into the courtyard.

▶ This delightful compact courtyard garden, seen here illuminated at night, was designed as an integral part of a house. The "room without a roof" is unusual in that it is not intended to be entered. Essentially a water garden, the space provides a restful extension to the adjoining living area when the doors are open.

oasis within the austere concrete-and-glass structure. The Matsushita Electronic Building in Shinagawa, Japan, designed by Nikken Sekkei and completed in 1996, is the company's centre for communications and information, and here the atrium fulfils a more abstract function. One of the objectives of the building's design was to express the company's credo of "harmony between humanity and technology."

The overall form of the building is a trapezoid. On either side of a central atrium are office blocks, the floors of which rise up towards each other to enclose the interior space and give the atrium a similar, trapezoidal shape. The west-facing end of the atrium is fully glazed, while the east-facing one is closed in by lifts and service facilities. Daylight enters the atrium through a narrow glass roof, and mirrors sited along the northern edge of the "roof light" reflect sunlight to

the floor of the space in winter. In summer the light is subdued by the filtering effect of the foliage of plants growing on the upper stepped floor shelves.

Reception and communal spaces are on the floor of the atrium, which also boasts a garden. Although Japanese in flavour, the garden has a contemporary feel to it and includes planting, abstract sculpture, and a waterfall. The atrium floor is divided into two zones, almost equal in size, consisting of an area of gravel and an irregularly shaped pool of water. Along the southern perimeter of the atrium the "floor" falls away to reveal a grassy slope leading to a subterranean stream. The gravel and water are crossed by stone paths and walkways that define routes to escalators and entrances. Two bridges of large stone slabs converge at the centre of the pool, one leading to a single-storey stone wall in which an opening gives

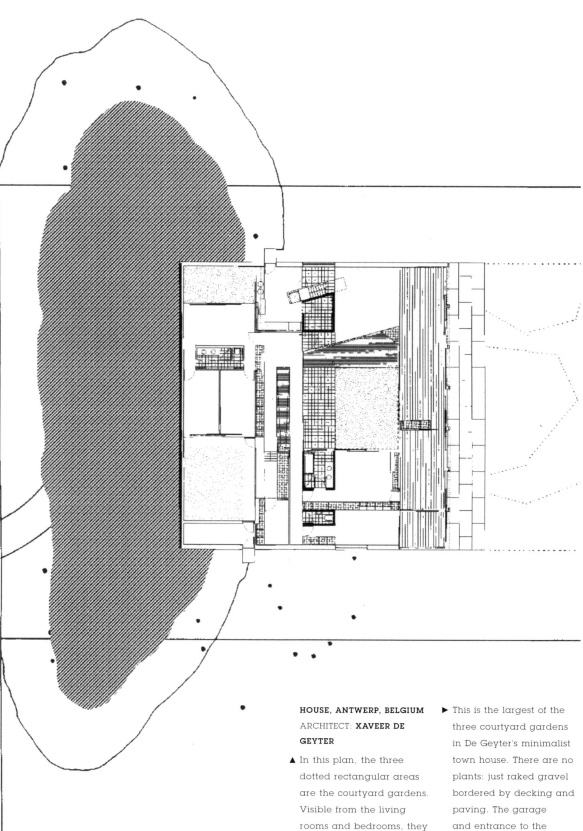

HOUSE, ANTWERP, BELGIUM
ARCHITECT: **XAVEER DE GEYTER**

▲ In this plan, the three dotted rectangular areas are the courtyard gardens. Visible from the living rooms and bedrooms, they give a sense of tranquillity.

▶ This is the largest of the three courtyard gardens in De Geyter's minimalist town house. There are no plants: just raked gravel bordered by decking and paving. The garage and entrance to the house are on the roof.

access to a lecture theatre. Water enters the pool via a stone incline that descends along the stone wall. The sound of the cascading water provides soothing background "music" and drowns out the noise of the building's ventilation system. The paths give human scale to the vast void of the atrium, and the natural stone surfaces and planted areas provide "earthy" contrasts to the towering architecture.

In recent years the architects and planners of large commercial developments have realized the need for sanctuaries of one kind or other within the workplace. By contrast, the home has always been a place where we expect to be able to escape the pressures of work, and the domestic garden, in particular, is a place of sanctuary. Most domestic gardens begin where the house ends. At the Shutters House in Los Angeles, California, the architects Moore Ruble & Yudell have created a garden space within the fabric of the building. The walls that surround it are part of the architecture of the house, and the height of the walls makes the space seem like a room. The floor of the garden consists of a shallow pool that "floods" a tiled floor. Emerging from the water in the pool are orderly lines of rectangular blocks of rough-hewn stone, but these are not intended as stepping stones, and only three larger slabs allow you to cross the water. The planting consists of a single clump of ornamental grass that rises from a square planter filled with pebbles. This water garden is not a place for activity but a private and intimate space, to be viewed and enjoyed from the glass doors that open on to it.

In the USA, Japan, and Europe contemporary domestic architecture has begun to challenge the conventional relationship between house and garden by integrating exterior and interior spaces. In the design for a house in Brasschaat, a suburb of Antwerp, Belgium, Xaveer De Geyter has even reconsidered the status of the garage. The house, with an area of 445 sq m (4800 sq ft), retreats into the ground and is hidden behind a sand dune that separates it from the street. De Geyter gives the car, a status symbol and essential of suburban life, a glass "temple," rather than an ordinary garage; this is situated on the entry-level roof. From the roof an entrance ramp, partly housed in a wedge-shaped tunnel, leads down to an enclosed "patio" garden and the main living quarters. In this house convention has been turned upside down: you descend below ground level to the garden, while the car is accommodated above.

The living room, dining room, and a bedroom open on to the garden. This Japanese-style courtyard, consisting of a covered deck, paving, and raked gravel, was conceived as an outdoor space rather than an ornamental garden. A planted garden would have been possible, but the architect preferred the minimal restfulness of raked gravel. The house even has a tea house for meditation.

The Ellison residence, in San Francisco, California, has a garden created by the American landscape architect Ron Herman. Completed in 1996, the area does not simply imitate the traditional Zen garden but transforms it. The result is an original, twentieth-century solution for a courtyard space of a recently modernized house.

The house has walls of glass and stainless steel and rooms that look out both over San Francisco Bay and inwards on to a central courtyard. The main access from the entrance of the property to living areas is via a glass-walled gallery that runs alongside the garden space. The client expressed an admiration for traditional Japanese gardens, and the design brief suggested that the garden should principally be one to be viewed rather than utilitarian. The design is based on the chequerboard patterned Zen garden at the Tofuku-ji monastery in Kyoto, which dates from the mid-seventeenth century. A superimposed grid defined by strips delineates the pattern. As the garden drops towards the north-east corner the bronze becomes more substantial and acts as a retaining edge to allow the grid pattern to become three-dimensional as it steps downwards. The planting is restricted to bamboo, dwarf *mondo* grass, and "baby tears" moss as ground cover. The bamboos are included to add interest to the tall, plain wall of one of the adjoining residences. The chequerboard effect is created by alternating squares of small, black, flat river pebbles and "baby tears" moss.

Although inspired by an ancient Zen garden, Herman's courtyard garden has little to do with religious devotion. In fact this modernist essay owes as much to Western minimalist art as it does to ancient Eastern culture. It is entirely in keeping with the uncluttered interior space of the house and the clean lines of the glass walls that overlook it.

At the Ellison residence the courtyard garden is separated from the house by the walls of glass and stainless steel, and access to the outdoor space is restricted to two doors. The need for a visual and physical separation of indoor living areas from outdoor space is challenged in the work of the Japanese architect Shigeru Ban, who is renowned for designing buildings that add contemporary twists to traditional Japanese architecture. In his design for the 2/5 House, in Tokyo – completed in 1995 – the architect returned to the long-established Japanese convention of linking interior and exterior spaces. However, he has done it in an exciting and radical new way, by considering the interior and the exterior as parts of the whole.

THE ELLISON RESIDENCE, SAN FRANCISCO, CALIFORNIA, USA
ARCHITECT: **RON HERMAN**
▶ This space, which is enclosed on two sides by the glass-and-steel walls of the renovated house to which it belongs, is also defined by the tall walls of the adjoining properties. It is a subtle essay in garden design that is restful to the eye and in contrast with the dynamic lines of the house.

◀ Herman's design for the
garden of the Ellison house
cleverly accommodates
the partly sloping site by
using a three-dimensional
interpretation of a
chequerboard pattern,
inspired by an historic
Japanese Zen garden.
The pattern formed by the
conjunction of squares of
pebbles – contained in
metal boxes – and moss
reveals an attention to
detail that lends this
garden a precious, almost
untouchable, quality.

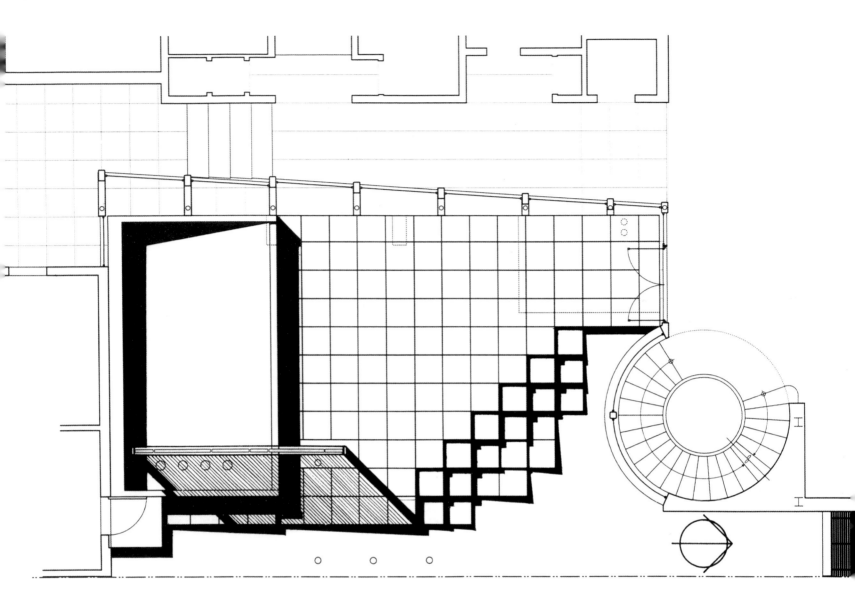

The rectangular plan of this house is divided into five zones, each 15m (49ft) by 5m (16½ft). Zone one includes a "front garden," which is concealed from the adjacent road by a perforated two-storey aluminium screen. Part of this screen can be folded up, like a venetian blind, to allow access to a garage. The second zone is an interior space, the third an open central courtyard, and the fourth a further interior space. The fifth contains entry steps and another exterior garden space, which is enclosed by an outer, two-storey screen covered in ivy. The five rectangular zones are bordered on their longer sides by concrete walls. Two enclosed glass "boxes" that span the second and fourth zones provide

accommodation on the second floor. Both boxes look down on to zone three, the central courtyard.

All the functional aspects of the house are on the ground floor. The fourth zone contains bedroom, bathroom, and a living-dining-kitchen area. Sliding doors, combined with an absence of vertical supports, allow each interior zone to open on to the front and rear garden spaces as well as the central courtyard. The latter has a tent-like roof which can be pulled out on tracks to provide shelter from inclement weather. When the doors are open the distinction between inside and outside, house garden and garden, is eliminated completely to provide one continuous living space.

▲ The schematic plan drawing shows the uncomplicated ground plan of the internal garden. On the left is the rectangular, raised, bronze-edged pool. On the right the checkerboard pattern of paving, pebbles, and moss steps down towards the spiral staircase. At bottom left, uniting these two main elements of the design, is the decorative glass screen.

For some designers the concept of a retreat has more to do with a plant and wildlife sanctuary than with a place devoted to peaceful contemplation. For them the ideal urban refuge is a green oasis in which plant life conceals bricks and mortar, and bird song drowns out the noise of town or city.

One such designer is the Frenchman Camille Müller, who is renowned for the courtyard and rooftop gardens that he has created for clients in Paris and New York. One of his most spectacular and unusual creations, however, is his own garden. Unlike his commissions, it lacks any formal plan and has instead evolved gradually, inspired by memories of his childhood spent in rural Alsace. Müller's home is in eastern Paris, within a courtyard, and here he has created a rural retreat that brings a strong sense of the country into the city. Although it might be described as a sanctuary, this garden is not intended as a place of rest or for passive contemplation. The designer regards it instead as a "place to garden, and to experiment with new ideas."

The main garden is on the inner, restored zinc-clad, V-shaped roof. The roof's structure was reinforced by a steel crossbeam, which is essential for it to support the wooden deck terrace and planted containers. Skylights give glimpses of this sunny

THE 2/5 HOUSE,
TOKYO, JAPAN

ARCHITECT: **SHIGERU BAN**

◄ The view from the bathroom
shows the central courtyard
on to which it opens. On
the far side of this simple
space is another living
area, which in turn opens
on to an enclosed garden.
Contained within the walls
of the house these exterior
areas are as private as
its interior spaces.

► This exploded drawing
shows the way in which
the architect has divided
the 2/5 House into five
zones. The two interior
living and sleeping areas
are sandwiched between
three enclosed exterior
zones. The zones are
divided by sliding glass
doors, which, when fully
opened, create a single,
uninterrupted space.

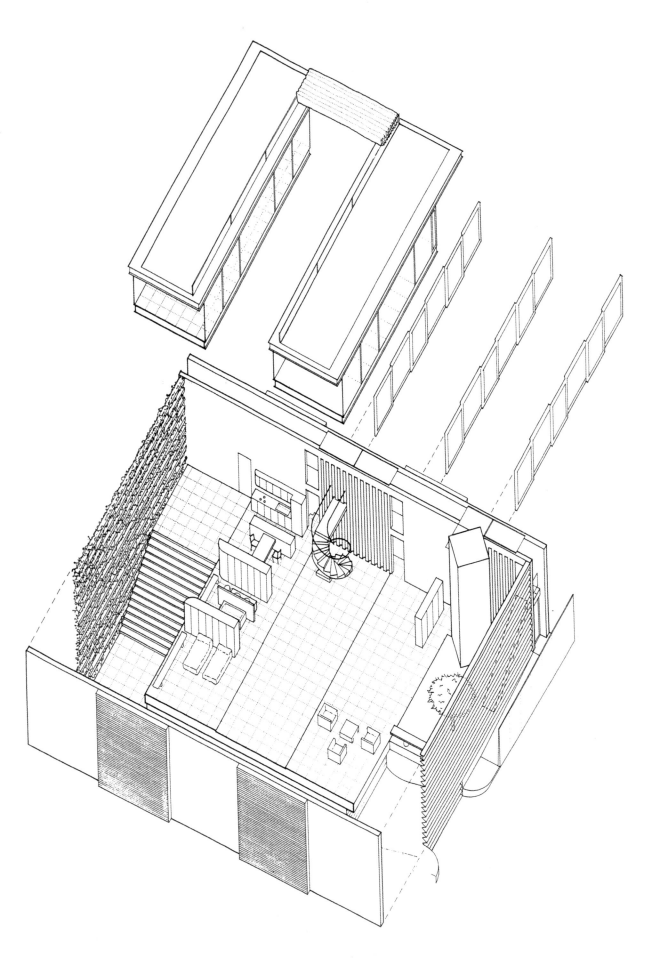

**COURTYARD GARDEN,
LONDON, UK**

DESIGNER: **LUCIANO GIUBBELEI**

◄ This tiny enclosed garden is
made to appear part of the
interior of the house by
the use of floor-to-ceiling
windows. The grid pattern
of the panes recalls a
Japanese paper screen,
and the oriental style is
continued in the simplicity
of the modern garden.

rooftop garden from below. The garden, with an area of about 100 sq m (1080 sq ft), is enclosed by walls and neighbouring buildings. Planted containers stand on terraced ledges which occupy three sides of the space. Other containers are fixed to the surrounding vertical walls. Boardwalks, metal steps, and ladders allow access to all areas and levels. The highest point, the only place from which the whole garden can be seen, is a metal platform that is reached only by a vertical ladder. As a result, house and garden are inseparable and interconnected. The apparently random mix of plants recalls a busy cottage garden, and

during the summer Müller has to work hard to prevent the space from becoming overgrown.

The creation of a sanctuary exclusively reserved for plant and wildlife is what the Japanese architect Kisho Kurokawa aimed to achieve in his design for Kuala Lumpur International Airport, Malaysia. This commission, completed in 1998, represents an attempt to realize his vision of an "Eco-media city," which he describes as a place where technology, nature, and society coexist in harmony.

To avoid an existing urban area, the site had to be cut out of a tree plantation that covered 1000

ROOF GARDEN,
PARIS, FRANCE

LANDSCAPE DESIGNER:
CAMILLE MÜLLER

▲ The difficulty in entering this green retreat above the city – it can be reached only by climbing out of the bedroom windows – is offset by the lush vegetation and the foodstuffs and kitchen herbs it produces.

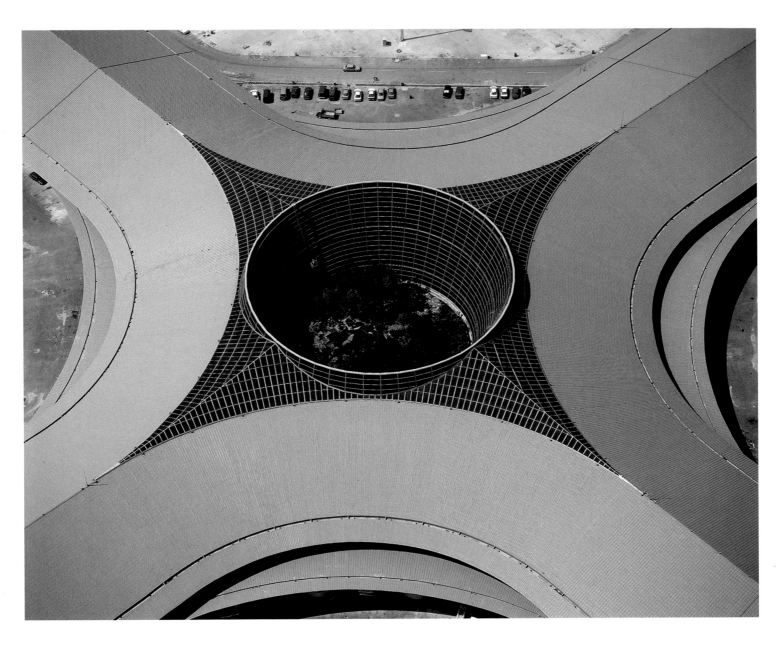

ARCHITECT: **KISHO
KUROKAWA**

▲ A man-made forest is
growing in the depths of
the Satellite Building, an
amphitheatre of steel and
glass at the airport's heart.
As the trees mature they
will become visible from
all the concourses.

hectares (2471 acres). Kurokawa, sympathetic to the
environmental impact on the young forest, has
established a new "forest" within the airport. At
the centre of the Satellite Building – the hub of the
airport's passenger circulation system – he has
inserted a circular void. This vast space is defined by a
towering, cylindrical, sloping wall of glass and steel,
but is open to the sky. Young trees and shrubs have
been introduced and these will, in time, become a
mass of abundant vegetation. The planting consists
mainly of indigenous species found in the Malaysian
rainforest and includes eighty-six species of trees,

thirteen kinds of palm, three types of bamboo, and a
wide variety of shrubs chosen for their large foliage.

The young pseudo-forest will be managed and
maintained as it grows, rather than being allowed to
develop in a more unpredictable, natural way.
Additional and replacement shrubs and trees are
being grown in the surrounding plantation. Although
the forest is visible from the surrounding airport
concourses, it is not accessible to the public. The
glass-and-steel wall serves to separate an interior
environment designed by technology from a man-
made, living external world. Such division implies a

desire to conserve and protect nature. But, ironically, an air traveller's view of this artificial forest is rather similar to that of a visitor at a zoo.

The opposite spatial relationship is encountered at the Sound Garden, designed by the artist Bernard Leitner. Here, the planting surrounds a cylindrical walled space. The garden, created in 1987, is situated within the Bamboo Garden, designed by Alexandre Chemetoff, in the Parc de la Villette, Paris. It consists of two concentric concrete cylinders, one inside the other. On the inner wall are eight grilles, each with eye-level slits through which water emerges and

falls in a "curtain" into a circular trough at the foot of the wall. Taped music issues from the grilles, filling the space with soothing sounds. The tops of the walls of the garden are level with the tops of the retaining walls and are surrounded by dense bamboos. The chamber may only be entered through narrow slits aligned on a north-south axis. The main route to the garden is via a long flight of steps, which descend through the bamboo grove to the garden's south entrance. The long, plant-lined approach and tall walls lend mystery to this secret garden. This is a walled garden with a difference – the plants are outside the walls.

SOUND GARDEN, PARC DE LA VILLETTE, PARIS, FRANCE
DESIGNER: **BERNARD LEITNER**
LANDSCAPE ARCHITECT:
ALEXANDRE CHEMETOFF

▲ Eight grilles in Leitner's concrete listening chamber emit both water and gentle recorded sounds to soothe visitors to this refuge set amid the tranquillity of Chemetoff's Bamboo Garden.

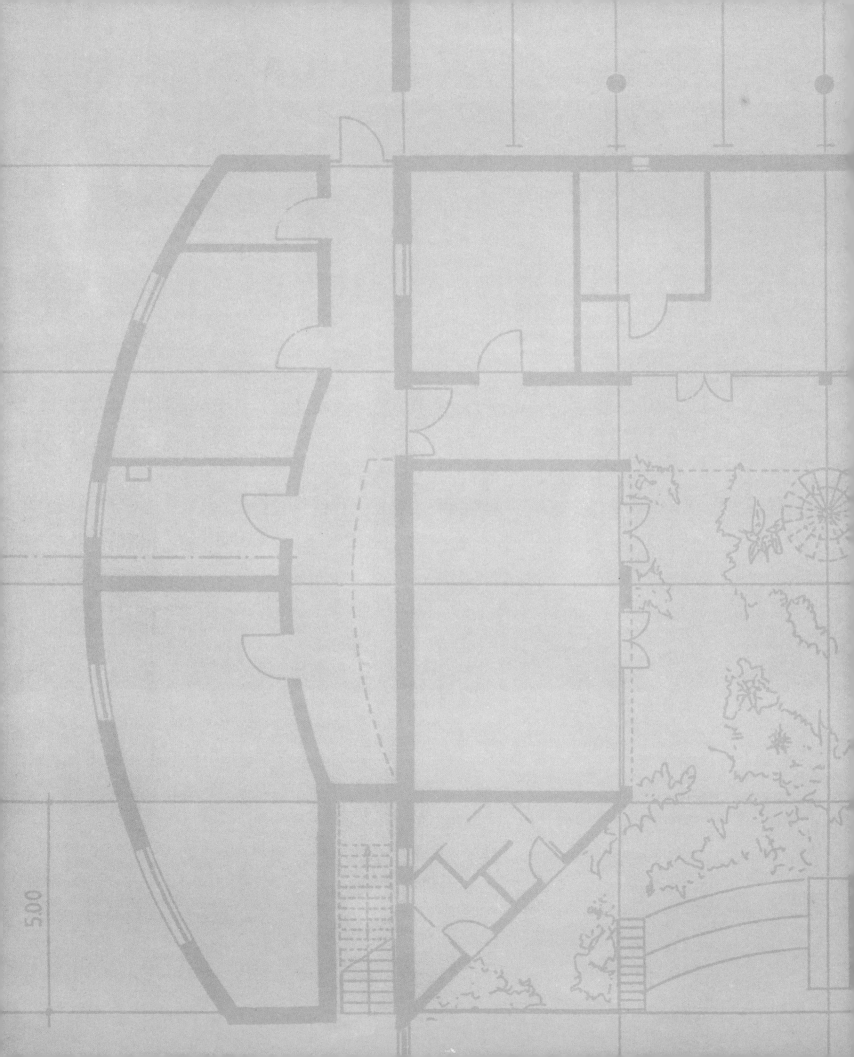

5.00

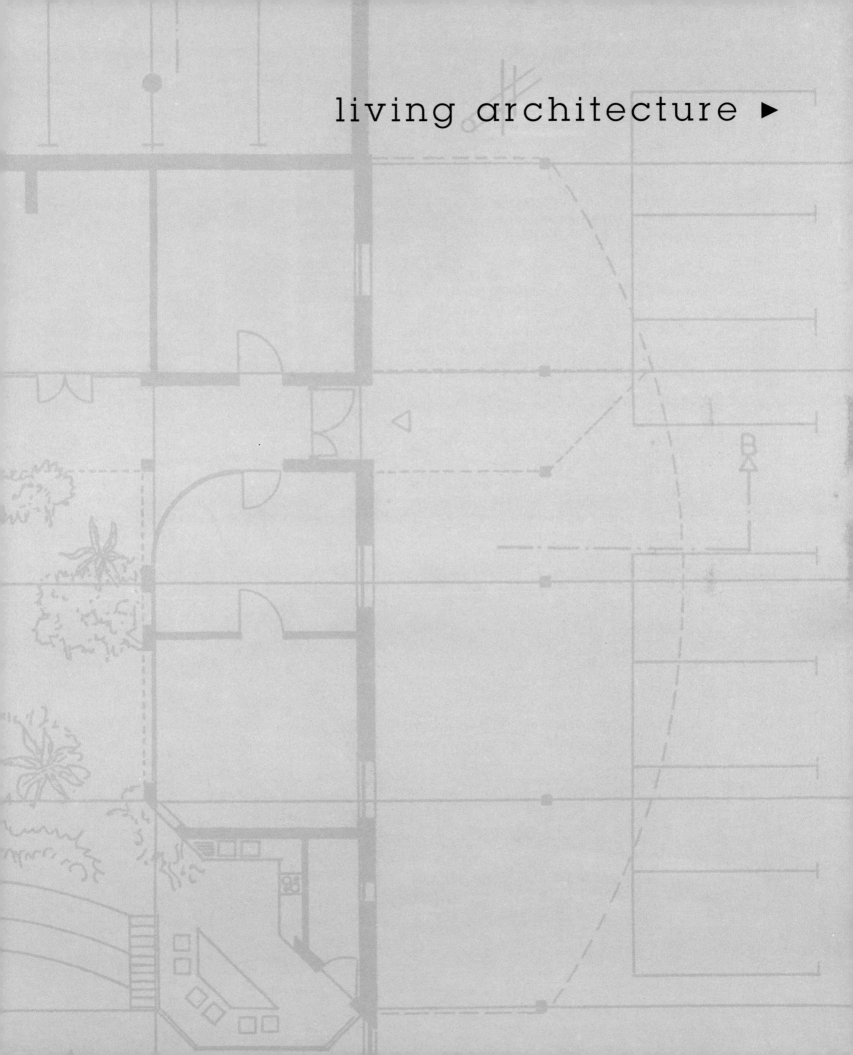

living architecture ▶

The term "living architecture" is used here to describe any building in which living, growing plants are included as essential and integrated elements within the fabric of the structure. Sometimes plants are employed to fulfil a precise function – for example, to improve air quality inside the building. In other instances the inclusion of plant material has a less specific role; it may be incorporated to make a building more environmentally friendly or to provide pleasanter working environment.

Many of the creators of "living architecture" consider this integration of vegetation and building essential if there is to be any improvement in the quality of life in towns and cities. The style has emerged since the early 1970s and particularly among developed countries, as a result of expanding social and political awareness of the importance of respecting our natural environment.

The origins of the environmental, or "green," lobby go back to the Arts and Crafts Movement of the latter half of the nineteenth century. William Morris, the predominant figure in this movement, was a poet, designer, and reformer. In his words and actions he developed and expanded the ideas of the art critic John Ruskin. A contemporary of Morris, Ruskin, in his book *Seven Lamps of Architecture*, had called for an architecture that was in sympathy with the order of nature. Morris, too, prized nature. He revered rural crafts, opposed the creations of the new mechanized age, and feared the consequences of urban industrial expansion. The concerns of Morris and other followers of the Arts and Crafts Movement went unheeded at the time, swamped by society's enthusiasm for the new industrial and machine era, which promised a better standard of living for all.

More than half a century passed before there was a marked renewal of concern for the environment. This change was heralded by the "Flower Power" movement of the 1960s, which promoted peace and love but, more significantly, introduced a renewed respect for nature. The movement advocated a lifestyle that was in harmony with nature and offered an alternative to what it saw as an uncaring world devoted primarily to commercial exploitation. In the following decade, as a result of disturbing evidence of

atmospheric deterioration provided by scientific studies that were monitoring the state of "planet earth," the Green Movement was born. Conservation of dwindling resources came to be seen as an urgent priority, and today there is widespread agreement that we ignore green issues at our peril.

Accelerating consumption of the world's natural resources is acknowledged as a problem, and buildings consume half of these supplies. Furthermore, they often house the activities that consume the remainder. Cities are not only the principal drain on these resources but are the main polluters of the environment. The architects Brian Edwards and Chrisna du Plessis, in an article in *Green Architecture*

"BIOCLIMATIC" SKYSCRAPER, SINGAPORE, MALAYSIA

ARCHITECT: **KEN YEANG**

▲ Ken Yeang's striking "bioclimatic" skyscrapers are characterized by their use of abundant vegetation. On every floor of this tower, slit-like recesses in the walls are filled with plants. The wall acts like a huge air vent, with the plants helping to improve the air quality both inside and outside the building.

▶ Schematic drawings of the building show how the planting, an integral and vital part of the design, spirals up the cylindrical structure. It begins as a turf mound that provides insulation for the lower floors and continues upwards as a series of gardens, described by the architect as "sky courts."

▼ A view from above a model of the proposed building shows a sun roof, consisting of a framework of steel and aluminium, designed to filter the light and provide shade for the swimming pool and gymnasium below. At the base is the grass mound that rises up and wraps around half of the circular tower's circumference.

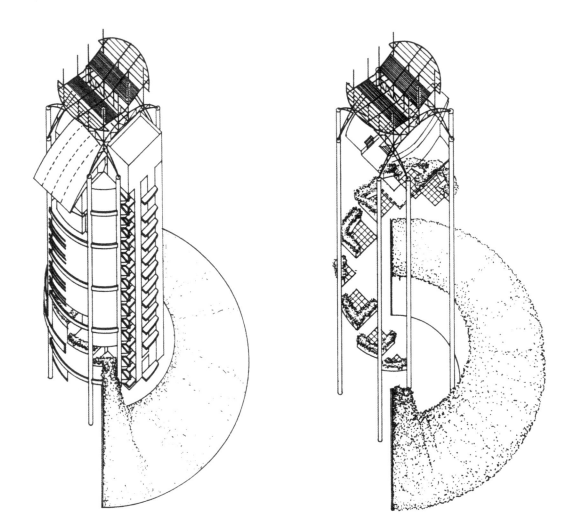

magazine, claim that "the inner life, not only of people but of cities, has suffered. In effect we have lost site of the building as a living thing."

Contemporary architecture is under pressure. Nearly all architects accept that today's buildings must take account of the scarcity of resources and the tendency of pollution to exacerbate climate change in an age when society is making ever-increasing demands on space. Yet at the same time we are reluctant to dismantle the idea of cities as the commercial and social centres of a nation. The problem of maintaining quality of life and the environment is provoking the need for innovative ideas in technology and architectural design.

Enlightened designers and architects have taken on this challenge, and many have looked to the natural world for solutions, sometimes drawing on its systems and processes, sometimes borrowing its forms and structures. In an interview for an issue of *Architecture Design* magazine that focused on green architecture, the Malaysian architect Ken Yeang expressed the view that "Nature should be imitated and our built systems should be mimetic ecosystems." He added that a "successful 'green' building is one that integrates seamlessly with the natural systems in the biosphere, with minimal destructive impact on these systems and maximum positive impact."

In his architecture Yeang enlists the help of nature in a direct way. He uses living plants both inside and outside his buildings as essential components within the overall design. For this architect, plants are not simply decorative extras. His incorporation of nature not only provides sensory pleasure for the building's occupants but also helps to cleanse the air.

The most common relationship between the two disciplines of architecture and landscape design is best understood by examining the distinction between them. The architect designs the building and defines its internal and external spaces. The landscape designer brings garden features and greenery to these predetermined spaces. Interior landscapes are frequently designed after the building is complete and are often an afterthought. However, there is a group of green architects, Yeang among them, who consider plants and gardens to be not simply a

MENARA MESINIAGA BUILDING, SELANGOR, MALAYSIA
ARCHITECT: **KEN YEANG**

▲ This skyscraper is slowly turning into a vertical garden, as the planting becomes established. In addition to its "bioclimatic" role of enhancing the air quality for the building, the spreading vegetation will gradually soften the high-tech exterior.

▶ In designing his high-rise buildings Yeang likes to designate floor space for air-cleansing gardens and terraces. On the roof of the Menara Mesiniaga Building he has installed a luxurious swimming pool, complete with changing room and a terrace garden. This attractive elevated space also affords spectacular views over Selangor.

decorative additions to buildings but essential parts of their fabric. These architects regard plants as vital ingredients in the "working" and "life" of the architecture. In effect, they design buildings that function as living organisms.

The Menara Mesiniaga Building, the Malaysian headquarters of the electronics company IBM, was designed by Yeang and completed in 1992. Situated in Selangor, it is one of a number of towers he has created for corporations and developers in the densely populated cities of the Far East. What makes Yeang's tall buildings distinctive is the innovative way in which he combines high technology with luxuriant vegetation and vertical planting. Fifteen storeys high and circular in plan, Menara Mesiniaga is constructed from industrial materials, such as glass, aluminium, and steel, that are associated with modern high-tech skyscrapers. But here, the materials have another function in addition to expressing a modern aesthetic.

For Yeang is a specialist in "bioclimatic" architecture. This term describes a type of building designed to combat environmental degradation. The Menara Mesiniaga Building was designed, both internally and externally, with this aim in mind, and the result is a structure that, in addition to consuming

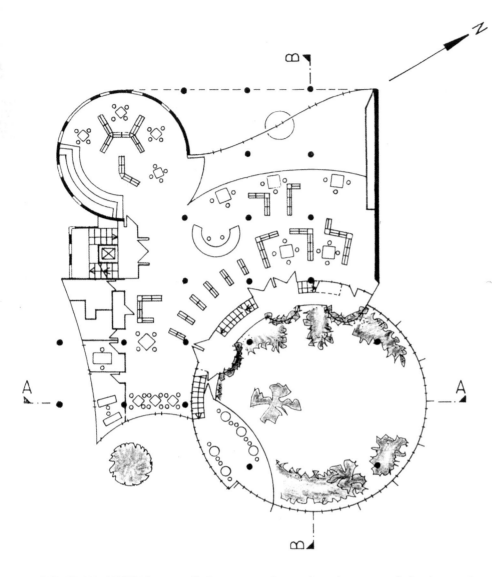

B

N

A — — A

B

LIBRARY AND CULTURAL CENTRE, HERTEN, GERMANY
ARCHITECT: **DIETER SCHEMPP OF LOG ID**

▲ The first-floor plan of the whole building shows how, in the rotunda, the ground-level planting is mainly at the perimeter, to allow space for events.

◄ With its containerized subtropical plants, this round garden under glass is a pleasant backdrop for the centre's activities. The garden has a further function in boosting oxygen levels as part of the building's air-conditioning system.

little energy, also makes the most of the hot and humid tropical climate of Malaysia.

The building's most distinctive feature is the abundant planting. Beginning on the ground floor, this vertical landscaping of turf and plants surrounds the main entrance and forms a mound that climbs to the third storey, providing insulation for the ground floor. The planting continues up the façade of the building, spiralling up to a rooftop terrace by way of a series of "sky courts." These recessed, three-storey high terraces, which provide rest and recreation areas for the staff, are also heavily planted. Resembling elevated atriums, they allow cool air to flow into the tower to support its own air-conditioning. For the benefit of the occupants, the planting in the "sky courts" provides essential shade and pumps additional oxygen into the local atmosphere.

In the densely populated cities of the Far East, where consumerism and economic growth have increased at an alarming rate, Yeang has enjoyed some success in introducing the politically sensitive issue of green architecture by disguising it within a fashionable architectural style. At the same time he has convinced clients of the economic benefits of energy-saving buildings.

One of the architectural practices most involved in living architecture is the German firm LOG ID. The company employs botanists as part of a team that also includes engineers, physicists, and medical doctors. It specializes in the use of green technology, and is spearheaded by Dieter Schempp and Dieter Wolter. Schempp, born in Stuttgart in 1944, studied at the technical college in Detmold. He formed the company in 1972, in partnership with Wolter, who also has a scientific background.

The initial aim of LOG ID was to develop energy-saving, solar-based construction methods that could be used in architecture. This application of "climate control technology" has since produced a series of "building-within-building" constructions, using a principle based on layers of walls. The walls are designed in such a way that they collect the sun's rays, allow temperature-controlled air to flow, and can incorporate living plants or whole gardens that help to refresh the air within the buildings.

The basic construction principle involves the use of an exterior glass enclosure, which consists of the outer walls and the roof. Within this enclosure is a well-insulated "core" structure. In winter the "building within a building" absorbs and retains the heat of the sun, which is then transferred throughout the rest of the building. In summer the system works in reverse: trees and plants in the spaces between the exterior glass walls and inner opaque walls offer shade. Through transpiration, the plants naturally increase humidity in the building, which also improves the air quality.

This approach was put into practice in LOG ID's design for the Research Laboratory for Experimental Traumatology at Ulm. Designed by Schempp and associate architect Fred Mollring, and completed in 1989, the building has a "core" structure that includes doctors' offices and consulting rooms, laboratories, and a library. These rooms all have windows and doors that open on to a greenhouse-like atrium with glass walls and sloping glass roof. This space, between the solid inner walls and the outer transparent glass membrane, houses the principal lecture theatre. To the rear of the stepped seating is a heavily planted garden of large foliage plants. Additional planting, mainly ivies, tumbles from containers set high on the back wall. The result is a work environment that is both practical and aesthetically pleasing.

In 1990 LOG ID employed a variation of this "greenhouse" system in its design for a printing factory at Lahr, in the Black Forest. The clients, Medium GmbH, required a building that would protect employees from the harmful chemicals associated with printing, but, at the same time, one that would demonstrate that the company was actively engaged with environmental issues. The result is a building in two halves: one half is used for production, the other is for administration; linking the two sections is a greenhouse, complete with a plant-filled garden. The structure provides solar heating, and the interior vegetation, clearly visible from outside, connects the building visually and psychologically to its immediate environment and the wider landscape.

RESEARCH LABORATORY TRAUMATOLOGY, ULM, GERMANY
ARCHITECTS: DIETER SCHEMPP AND FRED MOLLRING OF LOG ID

▼ In the lecture theatre, a dense planting of small trees and large-leafed evergreen shrubs provides a relaxing environment.

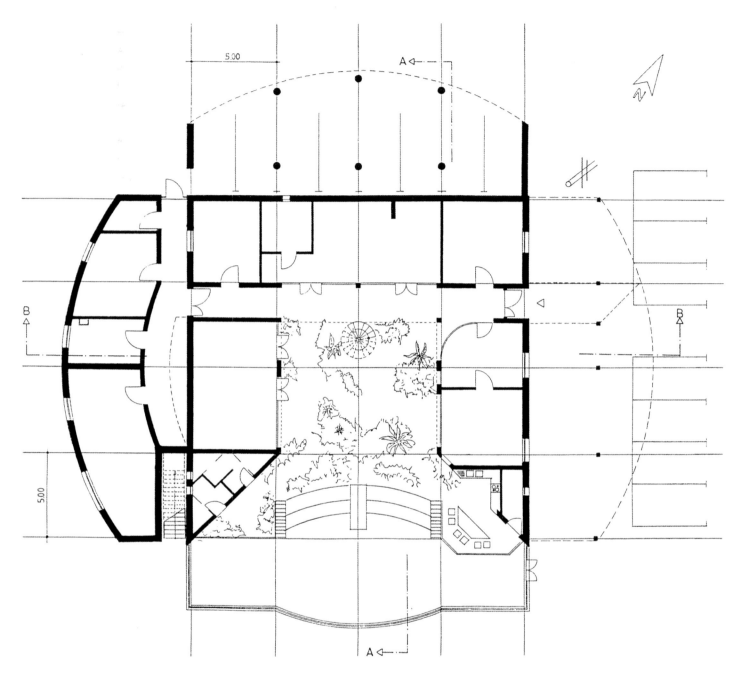

The most impressive building created by LOG ID to date is its "Glasshouse," in Herten, Germany. Designed by Schempp and Mollring and completed in 1994, it combines the functions of a library and a cultural centre and incorporates a multi-level garden. The building consists of two linked elements: a four-storey library block and a four-storey glazed, drum-like rotunda that serves as the cultural centre. Balconies open from the adjoining library on to the glass rotunda along a third of its circumference. Along the remainder of the circumference of this cylindrical atrium is a glazed external wall.

To make the most of the sunlight, the architects specified a large, multi-apex, glass roof. This zigzag structure, which projects beyond the vertical glass walls of the rotunda, acts as a vast solar collector. The heated air is circulated to warm the internal spaces. This system is supplemented by the use, in the library, of concrete walls and ceilings, which absorb the heat and maintain the interior at a comfortable temperature.

▲ The ground-floor plan of the research institute in Ulm shows offices, laboratories, and consulting rooms arranged around three sides of an atrium garden, which also contains the lecture theatre. The atrium's planting circulates rejuvenated air to the surrounding workplaces.

In summer the roof can be opened to allow warm air inside to rise and exit, which in turn draws in colder air at ground level. This process provides an efficient form of air-conditioning. In short, the cylindrical glass atrium acts as a vast solar collector, distributing warm air in winter and expelling heat, through ventilation, in summer.

Inside the glass rotunda the designers have created a spectacular, multi-level hanging garden. A ground-floor courtyard garden has been made using large, free-standing containers, some planted with tall-growing trees that will eventually reach the roof, others with large-leafed, subtropical shrubs. The garden continues upwards, with plants trailing down from troughs that project from the upper balconies. The vegetation enriches the air with oxygen and provides shade in summer. Plants are good absorbers of sound, and are therefore of further benefit to the library, as they reduce noise from outside. Within the multi-purpose space on the ground level of the rotunda the garden is a relaxing place where employees and visitors can sit. Externally, the building

rises like a great greenhouse out of the somewhat sterile townscape that surrounds it.

Since 1970 the German architect Thomas Herzog has combined in his work a rational, economic style of architecture and a commitment to ecological considerations. His commissions, which include many domestic houses, take into consideration issues such as climate, solar energy, and thermal technology. In the design of a house, completed in 1984 at Waldmohr, Germany, Herzog uses what he terms the "thermal onion" plan. In this system, which is similar to the one adopted by LOG ID, the rooms that need to be warmest, for example the bathroom, are placed in the centre of the building. These "warm rooms" are then surrounded by other rooms, the temperature of which decreases in proportion to their proximity to the outer skin. On the south-facing elevation Herzog has used both external and internal glass façades. A plant-filled conservatory between these transparent walls acts as a temperature-controlled buffer zone. In addition, a planted roof and a leafy trellis shade the east and west elevations.

HOUSE, REGENSBURG, GERMANY

ARCHITECT: **THOMAS HERZOG**

▼ A diagrammatic sketch of the energy-saving house shows how sunlight, which enters through the partly glazed roof, is used to warm the house in winter and keep it cool in the summer. In winter heat is retained within the building's core, while in summer the solar-based system circulates cool air.

▶ To each side of the main doors, at the outer edge of the glazed roof, plant-filled conservatories, which provide interior gardens, benefit from the southerly orientation. The whole structure is raised on stilts to prevent damage to the roots of the surrounding beech trees.

Earlier, in 1979, Herzog had created a similar "passive" solar dwelling at Regensburg. Like the house at Waldmohr, the building comprises a system of "layers," in which intermediate temperature zones are wrapped around a warmer core. The structure of the house is based on a simple wedge shape with a sloping roof. This south-facing roof is glazed to allow extra light into the interior, provide a source of solar energy, and form greenhouse-like enclosures, at its lowest point, which is at the front. Glass partitions and walls separate the lower, partly glazed, planted zone from the interior space of the house. This semi-external zone acts as the outermost layer, providing an indoor-outdoor space that is both architecture and garden.

Adopting a similar approach, LOG ID employed planting in a commission for a private residential scheme in the Swiss town of Biel. The building,

completed in 1993, contains eight dwellings: five two-storey apartments on the lower levels and three smaller, single-floor apartments on the top level. Each dwelling has a balcony, but it is the glasshouse situated on the front, south-eastern façade of each that is the most original feature of the scheme.

The glasshouses of the maisonettes are two storeys high, while those of the flats rise slightly above the roof level to gain maximum light. These "winter gardens" help to utilize the energy from the sun, and the main solar benefit is gained in the winter. At this time of year, on cold but sunny days, an inner glass partition between the rooms and the conservatories can be opened to allow warmth generated in the glasshouse into the interior. The inner concrete structure of the building absorbs this heat and – the reverse of a night-storage heater – keeps the living spaces warm at night.

APARTMENT BUILDING, BIEL, SWITZERLAND
ARCHITECT: **DIETER SCHEMPP OF LOG ID**

▲ The unusual three-storey glazed structures that dominate the sunny façade of this apartment building are part of a solar-powered heating and air-conditioning system. Within the indoor gardens formed by the glass walls, semi-tropical plants give shade and increase oxygen levels.

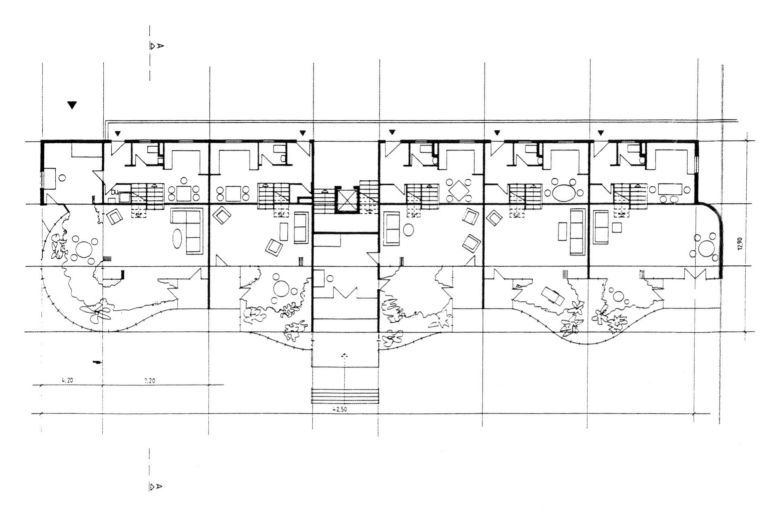

The planting in the glasshouses is by no means an afterthought. The semi-tropical plants are set in specialized sunken containers that run the full length of each of the curved-glass outer walls. In this way the plants are presented at floor level, rather than in the usual *ad hoc* arrangement of free-standing raised planters. This novel solution creates the impression of a real garden, and, when the glass screen between conservatory and living accommodation is open, the garden becomes part of the interior. As with other examples of green architecture, the plants, which are watered by a built-in automatic irrigation system, also serve practical purposes, namely to give shade and to raise oxygen levels.

STERN is another German company interested in environmental issues. Founded in 1978 and based in Berlin, it is committed to finding green solutions for urban redevelopment schemes. The group specializes in designing and coordinating alternative planning ideas for urban redevelopment schemes, including projects in the inner city, and is dedicated to seeking opportunities to introduce more plants and trees into towns and cities.

On commencing work on Block 103, a housing project in Berlin dating from the 1980s, STERN first spoke with the residents of the existing run-down block of flats to ascertain the sort of environment in which they would like to live. From the survey the company was able to establish what was required to humanize and improve the site, namely the introduction of greener technology and a greater emphasis on landscaping.

The new communal garden, which makes use of existing space within the site, has proved popular with the residents. The multi-storey terraced buildings function like the bricks and mortar of a walled garden,

▲ The floor plan of the apartment building in Biel reveals the design team's imaginative concept. Each of the eight apartments has a curved, glazed structure on its south-facing frontage. The glasshouse is separated from the rest of each dwelling by a glazed partition. Opening the partition creates a combined living room and conservatory and allows air heated within the glasshouse to permeate the rest of the apartment.

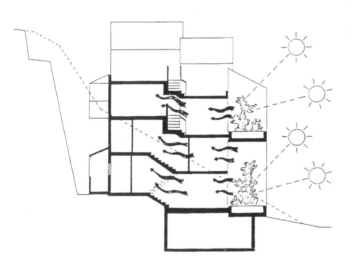

sheltering the inner secluded gardens. Pathways through the planted borders and across lawns link the properties, and there is plenty of space for recreation. Block 103 also has its own private park contained within its walls. STERN's original concept drawings suggest that planting was going to be used to cover and insulate roofs as well as to improve the appearance of walls. These ideas have not been fully realized but what has been completed and installed is the ingenious vertical Swamp Garden.

This feature is secured to the end wall of a row of houses and uses technology and the properties of certain plants to clean and recycle used water. Although the device cannot treat sewage water or produce drinking water, it allows water from the bath and kitchen to be reused. This climbing bog garden depends on a number of large, open-ended, green plastic barrels, secured at different levels of the wall within a tubular-steel, scaffold-like frame. Plants that like damp or swampy conditions are placed in the containers, which are partly filled with a moisture-retentive, gravel-based planting medium. Used water from the row of houses is delivered to the containers, and it passes slowly through each level of the vertical garden it is gradually purified by the plants to provide reusable, non-drinking water. Aquatic and marginal plants that are very efficient at cleansing water include *Phragmites communis*, *Carex pendula*, *Iris pseudacorus*,

Polygonum amphibium, and *Typha latifolia*. Many of them are floriferous and contribute to an unusual garden that is not only functional but also aesthetically pleasing.

For decades architects and planners have addressed the problems of urban decay, with mixed results. Ecological and sustainable architecture that is both affordable and attractive to the populations it serves has found little favour in Britain. Its planners lag far behind their counterparts in, for example, Germany and the Netherlands, in grasping what opportunities there are, particularly in the heart of the cities, and in encouraging those with the vision to produce such housing. The possibilities for innovation have been limited, and the problem is not just confined to the city. Suburbia, with its sprawling, low-density housing, makes great demands on land, often "greenfield" sites, and consumes excessive energy per capita. Unfortunately, social aspirations, coupled with a deep attachment to the car, run counter to the search for an alternative to the current wasteful suburban culture; nor is there much political will for change.

However, a vision for a new type of suburb is at last being realized in the UK. The Beddington Zero Energy Development, or BedZed, in the London Borough of Sutton, is a purpose-built housing project. Designed by Bill Dunster Architects and begun in 2000, it demonstrates that new solutions can be found to the problem of improving the quality of urban life. On the unpromising site of a former sewage-treatment plant, this scheme, ecologically driven and less resource-consuming than conventional schemes, is taking shape. Supported and supervised by the Peabody Trust Housing Association and the environmental charity BioRegional, BedZed is an attempt to establish a sustainable, high-density community that combines living and working space, shops, a health centre, nursery, and sports club.

Dunster's team of architects have turned for their inspiration to the post-industrial urban terrace, or row, housing, but have considered it in a new way. In this scheme the basic living module is a three-storey townhouse, which can be used for single occupancy or divided into separate flats to provide low-rent social housing. Despite the high density of the development – fifty dwellings per hectare (2½ acres) – the terraces boast balconies, all have self-contained roof gardens, and the single-ownership properties also have conventional back gardens.

The team involved in the project have shown that a garden, which most people regard as necessary for personal well-being, can be provided for all. They have achieved this by integrating the garden into the design as simply another "room" within the confines of the architecture, rather than treating it as an afterthought or something to be made available only to the privileged.

The pursuit of green engineering and technology has led some architects to incorporate living plants as essential ingredients in the functioning of their

"SWAMP GARDEN," BLOCK 103, BERLIN, GERMANY

DESIGNER AND CONTRACTOR: **STERN**

◄ An unconventional water garden is suspended from the south-facing end wall of a row of inner-city houses. The Swamp Garden is one of the most innovative features of an ecologically inspired scheme for renovating homes in a high-density urban environment.

▲ Both functional and aesthetic, this vertical garden creates a verdant living wall as well as emphasizing conservation of water by recycling it for washing and cleaning.

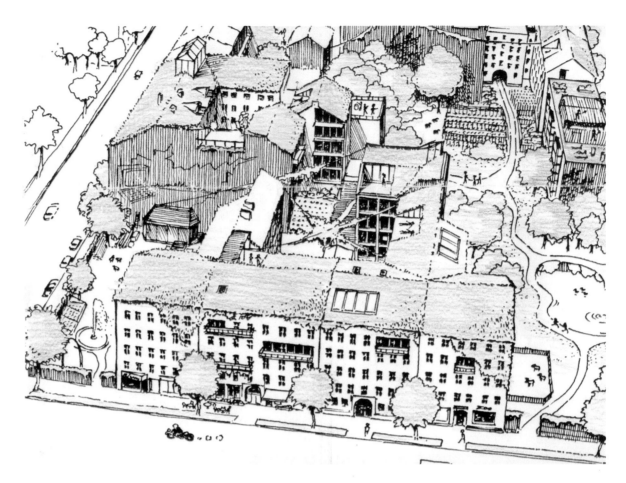

▶ This sketch for the revitalization of Block 103, in Berlin, shows formerly derelict urban housing reclaimed to provide high-density living space in a green landscape. Planting has taken over the rooftops, and the area is now like a public park, with fountains, duck ponds, and tree-lined paths.

buildings. For another group, vegetation and even the ground in which it grows have been incorporated as architectural elements to create buildings that are fusions of landscape and architecture.

Arthur Quarmby was one of the first modern architects to create earth-sheltered structures. It was in the 1970s that he began his pioneering experiments in below-ground construction and earth-covered housing. Most of his completed underground buildings are sited in rural England, although one of the main advantages of a roof constructed of sods of earth is that it can provide temperature insulation in desert environments.

Despite his earlier interest in high technology, Quarmby has been attracted by the architecture of earlier civilizations, such as Hindu religious shrines in India and the Bronze Age earth-covered shelters of ancient Britain. The common factor is a method of construction that requires carving into the land, rather than building on top of it.

As populations continue to grow, with demands for housing putting pressure on undeveloped "greenfield" sites, Quarmby's architectural vision offers a resolution of the conflict between conserving nature and providing homes. In conventional architecture the exterior of the building is designed to make a visual impact. Quarmby's idea is to make "invisible architecture" that combines habitat with the existing topography so that his designs are indiscernible within the landscape.

The aptly named Underhill House was Britain's first modern earth shelter, dug deep into a sloping hillside. In the below-ground house that Quarmby built for his own family in Yorkshire, light enters through skylights set into the living roof, which has evolved into a microcosmic nature reserve.

Quarmby's architecture is as much about the trees and plants that cover the building as the man-made materials that form it. He goes further than simply blending architecture into the natural environment.

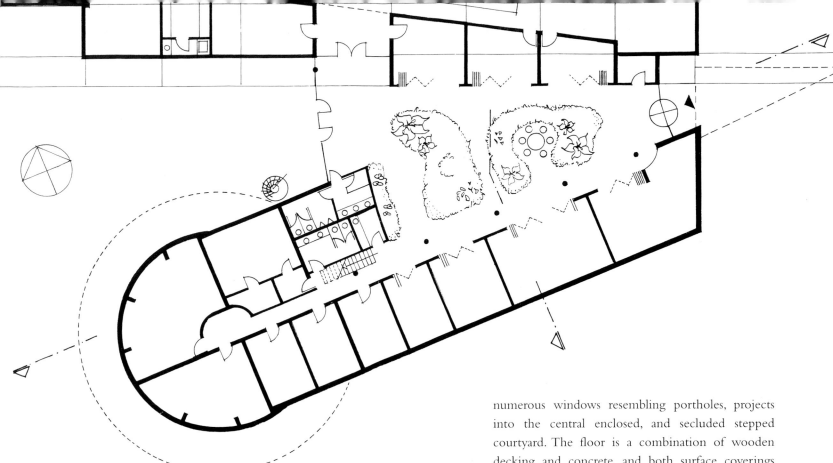

MEDIUM GMBH PRINTING
FACTORY, LAHR, GERMANY

ARCHITECT: **DIETER
SCHEMPP OF LOG ID**

◄ The plan drawing
shows how the architect has
split the building with the
wedge-shaped greenhouse
and garden. Offices in the
administration wing open
directly on to the garden.
The planted areas are
organic in shape and
contrast with the building's
triangular geometry.

▲ A view into the glass
greenhouse, which
separates the factory's
production area from
the administration wing.
The garden is visible from
outside and so helps to
integrate the factory into
its natural surroundings.

The architect adopts what he calls "over-the-top landscaping" to create new, vegetation-covered landscape features.

Whereas Quarmby has dealt with rural locations, a Japanese and a Scottish architect have joined forces to develop an organic architecture for urban situations. The husband-and-wife team of Eisaku Ushida and Kathryn Findlay, founded in 1988, has established a reputation for domestic architecture based on two environmentally friendly principles. They believe that a building should acknowledge the local topography and, without rejecting modern building technology, aim to create houses that suggest places of habitat, offering shelter and retreat, rather than ostentatious palaces. To this end their buildings are not imposed on the landscape or built environment but sit within it and are extensions of it. They see their role as "taming technology, not the taming of nature."

In the Ushida Findlay Partnership's Soft and Hairy House, built in 1994 for a young couple in Tsukuba City, near Tokyo, the building is dominated by organic shapes that form a warren-like enclosure. A bright-blue building in the form of a dome, with numerous windows resembling portholes, projects into the central enclosed, and secluded stepped courtyard. The floor is a combination of wooden decking and concrete, and both surface coverings continue into the interior, visible through the courtyard's glass doors and floor-to-ceiling windows. In the courtyard, planting is restricted to climbing plants and a single tree.

The most environmentally friendly feature of the house is the roof, which is topped by garden. The use of turf as an insulating material for roofs dates back many centuries. In Norway, for example, the builders of traditional cottages relied on it for protection from the harsh winters. In the warmer climate of Tokyo the planted roof of the Soft and Hairy House serves a different purpose. It insulates the house from the summer heat in order to maintain an acceptable room temperature. The extensive, informal roof garden of mainly indigenous planting tumbles over the outer and inner walls. As well as contributing to the thermodynamics of the house, it also provides an outdoor area for relaxation or entertainment that saves valuable ground space in this crowded city.

Sometimes the fusion of architecture and landscape is forced on the designer by the limitations of the site. An example is the Hanegi Forest apartment building in the Tokyo suburb of Setagaya-Ku. Designed by the Japanese architect Shigeru Ban

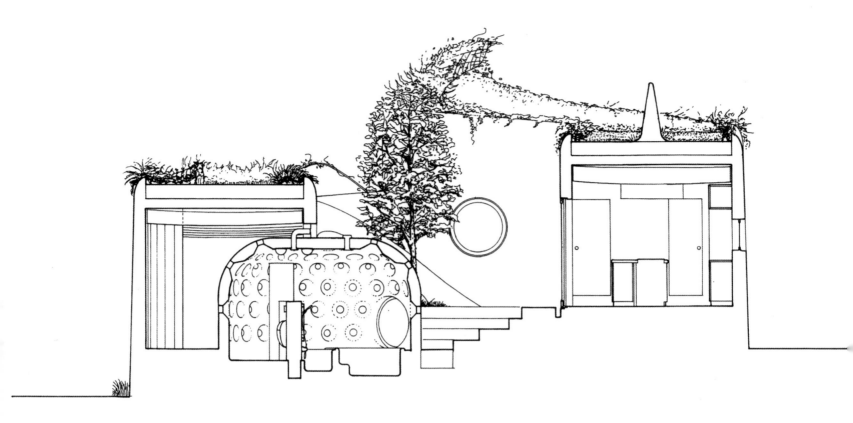

and completed in 1997, the apartment complex was constructed on a site that was home to twenty-seven mature trees of mixed varieties, all of which had to be retained and preserved. Even the building process could damage the trees, so a steel-frame method of construction had to be devised in order to minimize the amount of excavation.

Although Ban studied architecture at the Cooper Union school in New York, he returned to Japan to set up his own practice immediately after graduating. His work is characterized by its alternative construction methods and use of unconventional building materials. His ideas are founded on a deep respect for the history of Japanese architecture with its sensitive regard for the landscape. In many cases Ban's approach is dictated by the restrictions of the site, as with the Hanegi Forest apartments. Here, he chose, he says, to "interpret the circumstances and context of the particular site, discover an appropriate geometry, and extract from it a structure and space."

The random positioning of the trees ruled out the use of a box-like post-and-beam construction system – to accommodate them would have involved so many variables that the building costs would have

exceeded the budget. Instead Ban chose a triangular grid system that did not interfere with the trees. The eleven apartments are within a series of three-storey terrace houses with floor-to-ceiling windows that provide uninterrupted views of the trees surrounding them. Mirrors placed in the apartments are intended to enhance the sense of being in a forest.

Most of the trees that stand within the confines of the building are housed in elliptical voids that begin at ground level and continue upwards to pierce the gently pitched roof. Some of the voids are completely contained within the framework of the building, while others cut through the exterior walls of the apartments, with the ellipse truncated by the outermost building line. In one corner a first-floor circular deck projects to "grab" one of the trees.

The voids containing the trees are accessible at the level of the ground-floor entrance. The upper portions of their walls are clad with translucent glass blocks, which, although not completely clear, do allow the outline of the trees to be seen. In summer the canopies of the trees modulate the sunlight to project ever-changing patterns of light and shade on to the curved glass walls. The effects are clearly visible

THE SOFT AND HAIRY HOUSE, TSUKUBA CITY, JAPAN
ARCHITECTS: **THE USHIDA FINDLAY PARTNERSHIP**

▲ A cross-sectional drawing shows the proposed landscape features. An enclosed courtyard is to be minimally planted with a single specimen tree and climbing plants, while the main garden is to be located on the roof. This principal garden is shown here to be an integral part of the roof structure, for which it will act as an insulating membrane.

▶ The enfolding roof garden is informally planted, and the well-worn path is simply turf. Skylights and sculptural chimneys add to this unusual fusion of house and landscape.

from the adjacent apartments. Balconies open on to these spaces, and, in some instances, wooden decks wrap round and partly define the elliptical space at first-floor level.

Ban has provided the apartment complex with gardens by a process of adoption. The advantage of the site was that the trees were already established specimens. The occupants therefore had instant gardens, whereas normally it is years before a newly planted landscape becomes established and its benefits can be fully appreciated.

One of the architects most responsible for the development of environmental architecture, in which vegetation and terrain are integrated into buildings, is Emilio Ambasz. The Argentinian-born architect is also a respected industrial designer and established himself as an innovator in green architecture and design in the 1970s. In those early years his ideas for an urban utopia based on Arcadian principles met with indifference from both prospective clients and the architectural community, and as a result many of his projects were cancelled.

During the 1980s, however, attitudes changed and environmental issues became a pressing concern. By 1995 Ambasz had realized his most ambitious urban project with the completion of the ACROS Building, in Fukuoka, Japan. As a centre for international culture and information, this building accommodates conferences and exhibitions as well as theatrical and musical performances.

The fifteen-storey structure is as near a realization of the real or mythical Hanging Gardens of Babylon as can be found anywhere. The principal elevation is a multi-storey terrace of vegetation. The public gardens that lie in front of the building are not interrupted by it but appear to continue upwards, ascending its face like the cultivated terraces of the "lost cities" of the Incas in South America.

The ACROS Building achieves the central ambitions of green architecture in its use of environmentally friendly technology. What is more distinctive about this project, however, is the way in which the landscape has become an integral part of the building rather than simply a setting for it. In this aspect of the project Ambasz acknowledges a debt to

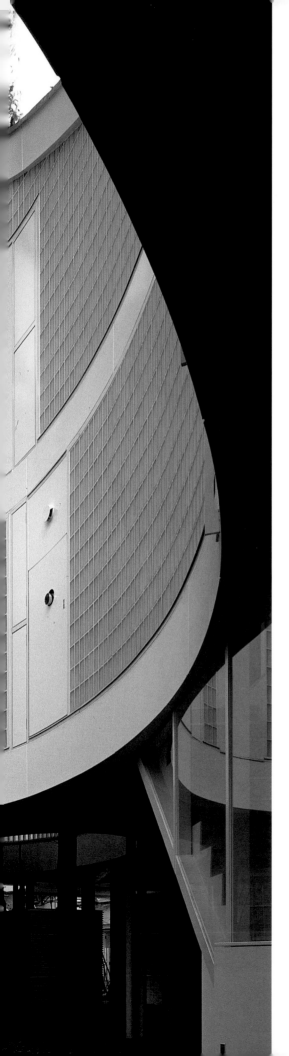

HANEGI FOREST APARTMENT BUILDING, TOKYO, JAPAN
ARCHITECT: **SHIGERU BAN**

◄ Two mature trees are accommodated in one of several three-storey voids designed to preserve a woodland within this apartment house. The entrance lobby apart, the ground floor is left as the original woodland floor, with the existing trees giving each apartment a self-contained garden.

▼ An exploded drawing indicates how the elliptical voids that accommodate the trees were developed as external living spaces, with decked terraces and staircases that lead up through the trees' canopies.

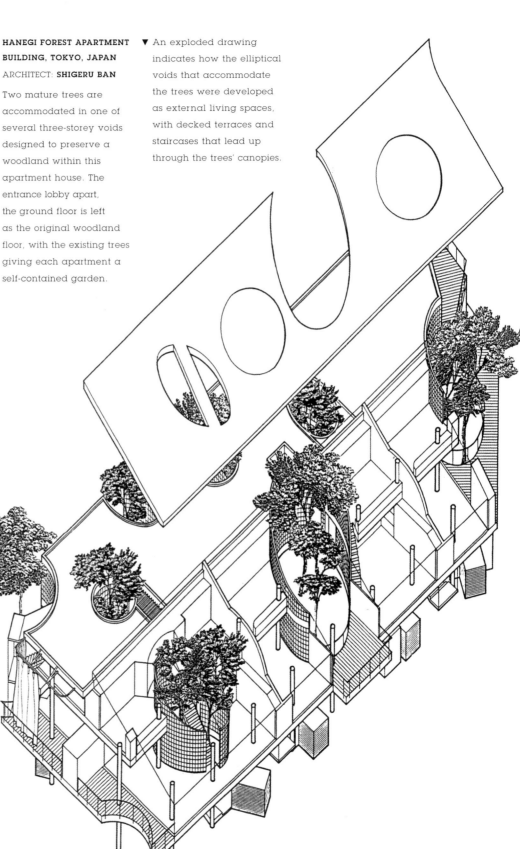

the American architect Frank Lloyd Wright. However, while Wright saw plants and landscape as essential adjuncts to his buildings, often "borrowing" the existing landscape, Ambasz uses architecture to create a new context for planted and living landscape.

Those who use the building reap the benefit of Ambasz's commitment to nature. The vast, terraced gardens can be used to take exercise or for sitting and relaxing. In the densely populated cities of Japan, where every piece of available space is exploited to meet human requirements, the building both serves the needs of society and provides nature with a placein which to flourish. In addition the plants provide a home for wildlife. In many ways Ambasz has revived the early twentieth-century concept of the garden city, in which nature was invited to share space with human activity and to contribute to the quality of suburban life. In this sense the ACROS Building is perhaps the ultimate garden city.

The role of the garden in society over the centuries has been diverse, and living architecture identifies a new role. Whether as a planted interior or a rooftop landscape, this genre is likely to become a major contributor to the development of sustainable and environmentally friendly buildings.

THE ACROS BUILDING, FUKUOKA, JAPAN

ARCHITECT: **EMILIO AMBASZ**

◀ Only from this viewpoint, looking towards the main elevation, can the effect of the planted terraces be fully appreciated. Covered with a mass of vegetation that leaves only the atrium visible, the building has become a vertical garden. It is one of the most impressive examples of green architecture created to date.

▼ A cross-sectional drawing illustrates the construction method used to create the planted terraces. The building was turned into a man-made mountain, with rock replaced by a steel framework. The angular, stepped, internal structure was transformed into a more natural-looking, irregular profile with layers of landscaping and planting.

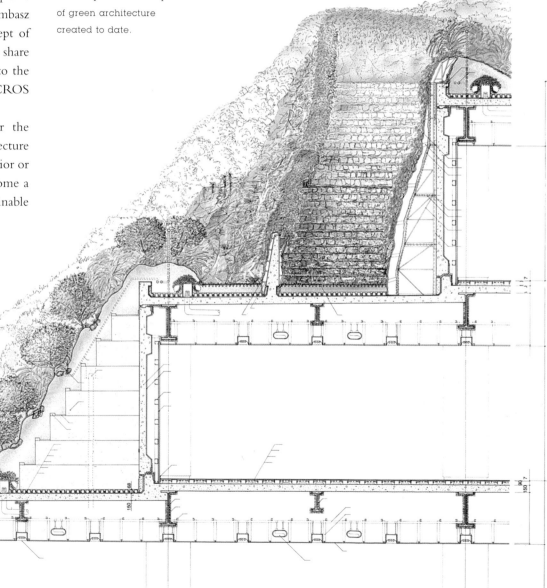

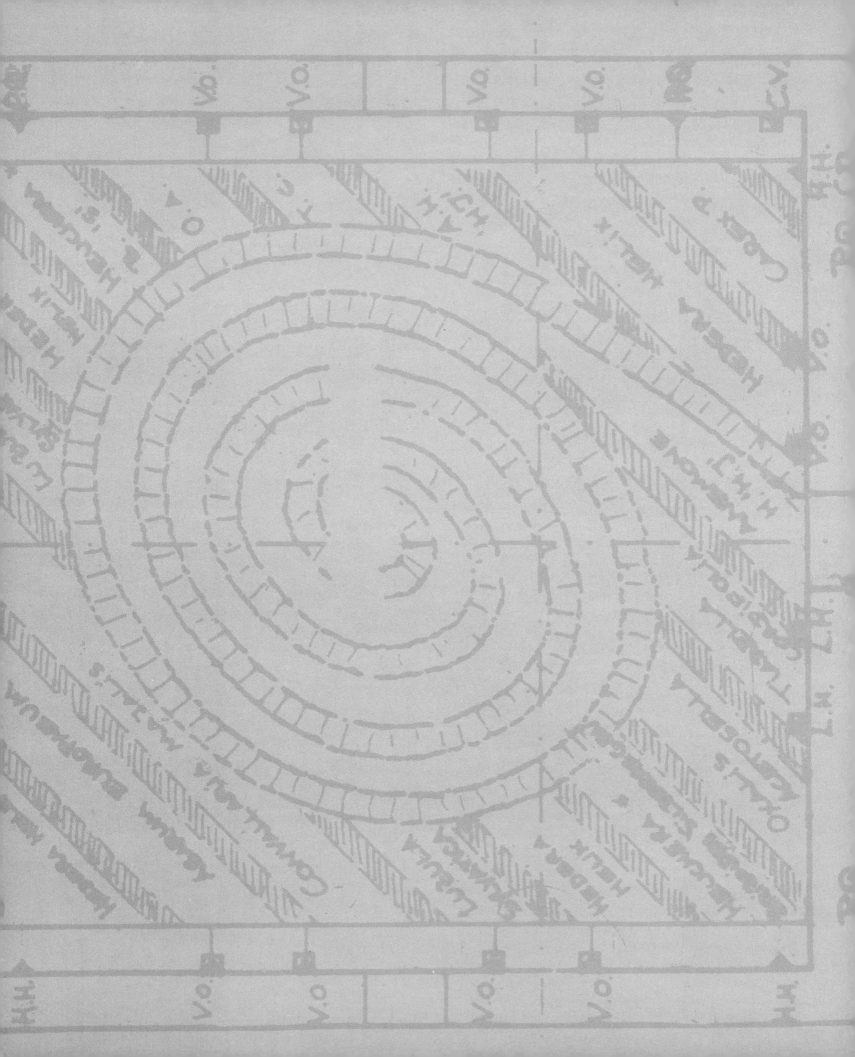

off the wall ▶

The relationship between a traditional garden or landscape and a building is most often one in which the architecture is adjacent to, or surrounded by, a garden or landscape. As we have seen, among the alternatives to this arrangement are gardens within buildings, such as those in courtyards or atriums. Gardens have also been sited on rooftops, although recently there have been instances where the association between garden and building has been much less orthodox, and landscape and garden features have appeared in the most surprising locations. This chapter looks at examples that are "off the wall" – most in the literal sense but some figuratively too – many of which were created by artists and sculptors rather than architects or landscape designers.

One such artist is the Israeli Dani Karavan. He specializes in art that makes a social comment and often creates environmental "installations," rather than single pieces of sculpture, to express his ideas. This is evident in a temporary work called "Mimmamakin," meaning "from the depths," which he created in 1997 in the abandoned buildings of a disused coal mine at Gelsenkirchen, in Germany. Carefully heaped piles of coal, redundant pieces of equipment, and pictures of former mine workers are orchestrated to conjure memories of times past. The scene is brought to life by special effects, including water, sound, and smoke. From the heaps of coal and disused tanks emerge plants – incongruous tropical palms and orange and olive trees – to suggest a garden. These exotic plants, normally associated with a sun-filled, serene, non-industrialized world, perhaps suggest a need to return to nature when seen in a landscape scarred by an industry that had scant regard for either plant or human life.

Modernist architecture has also attracted those who seek to create a green environment. Distinguished by its plain, unadorned appearance, the style has persisted in one guise or other since its emergence in the early twentieth century. Plants and trees have frequently been used as foils to the geometric regularity and the lack of surface decoration associated with these concrete, steel, and glass constructions. The German Chancellery building in Berlin is no exception. Completed in

"MIMMAMAKIN,"
GELSENKIRCHEN, GERMANY
ARTIST: **DANI KARAVAN**

▶ At a disused coal mine, palm trees sit in steel tanks, as if on a production line. This evocative tableau is part of a multi-media art installation by Karavan. Theatrical effects, such as synthetically generated smoke picked out by shafts of light, recreate the atmosphere of a working industrial environment.

▲ A detail of the façade of a factory renovated as a museum and art gallery dedicated to the work of Hundertwasser. A tree grows from one of the windows of the frontage, which was designed by the artist. Hundertwasser wanted to accommodate nature in his buildings, and one of his most radical yet simple ideas was to plant trees within rooms.

2001, the Chancellery, designed by the architects Axel Schultes and Charlotte Frank, contains landscaped courts and halls, but a more unusual feature greets arriving statesmen and civil servants. A group of free-standing, white-concrete columns stand like sentinels outside the entrance to the main building. These are not classical forms. Their shape, in section, is not circular but organic and asymmetrical, and in elevation, the tops are irregular. Whereas a classical column might be topped with a capital decorated with carved acanthus leaves, these ones have living plants at their summit, and huge pear trees grow out of some. Others are planted with moss, which will creep down the sides. The tall columns reach almost to an upper open terrace high above the entrance, and this allows the tree canopy to become an integral part of the upper level space as well.

Unconventional though planted columns or tree towers are, their impact on the architectural whole is minimal compared with the planted buildings of the eccentric artist/designer known as Hundertwasser, who was born Friedrich Stowasser in Vienna in 1928 and died in 2001. Finding himself at odds with

mainstream modernist architecture, he preached and practised an alternative style in which plants are as important as bricks and mortar.

Hundertwasser started his career as a painter and graphic artist. Although his work is collected and acknowledged internationally, it was his behaviour that made him a celebrity. From the late 1960s he organized public demonstrations and presented manifestos – sometimes in the nude – on architecture and environmental issues. In doing so he anticipated the modern green movement.

He had always been interested in architecture, and some of his early paintings depicted buildings, including skyscrapers, and had disconcerting titles such as "Bleeding Building" and "Pissing Boy with Skyscraper." His more recent architectural schemes, with their use of coloured tile mosaic, curvilinear walls, and exotic decoration, are in some ways similar to the work of the earlier Spanish architect Antonio Gaudí. However, Hundertwasser's desire to create a green architecture belongs firmly in the present, and most of his realized projects were completed in the last decade of the twentieth century. To build had been his ambition since the 1960s. For him the priority of a building is to protect, to be a "secure cave." His architectural visions studiously avoid technology and engineering, with grass roofs preferred to those built from steel and glass. Rebelling fiercely against what he regarded as the anonymous uniformity of modernism and the autocracy of the architect, he wanted buildings to have character and made personalized windows important features of those he designed.

In July 1983, at the International Gardening Exposition in Munich, Hundertwasser presented his manifesto "Concrete Utopias for the Green City," in which he demanded a "peace treaty with nature." This included giving back to nature architectural "territories" such as roofs, terraces, and other horizontal surfaces. What was needed, he said, was an "architecture doctor" who could "heal sick houses," and, logically, he appointed himself to the position.

Hundertwasser's "medication" included planting trees and woodlands on roofs and terraces and creeping plants on walls. His quickest and most

"PARK UP A BUILDING,"
SANTIAGO DE COMPOSTELA,
SPAIN
ARTIST: **VITO ACCONCI**

◄ Our normal perception of the public park is challenged by the vertical orientation of this portable and reusable modular recreational area made from steel, aluminium, and trees.

▼ The steel decks, seating, and trees of the "park" are supported by the horizontal arms of aluminium bars that are attached to the wall of the building. Diagonal stainless-steel wires give extra strength to the bars, which are adjustable in length and therefore can be used on walls of various heights.

surprising solution was the introduction of "tree tenants," an idea that he had first proposed in 1973 as his contribution to the Triennial Art Exhibition in Milan. The project required the transplanting of twelve trees from a woodland plantation into apartments on the city's Via Manzoni. The trees were lifted by cranes into the upper flats, and their roots were planted into sealed, soil-filled rooms. The canopy of the trees projected through open windows, and the roots were watered by diverted drainpipes. In 1980 a similar installation was made in a building on Alserbachstrasse in Vienna. Hundertwasser told the residents of the advantages of their new "neighbours," proclaiming each to be "an ambassador of the forest" able to produce oxygen, improve the local climate, filter toxic dust, absorb street noise, and attract bird life.

In 1991 he collaborated with the architect Peter Pelikan to turn a former furniture factory in Vienna into the KunstHausWien. The renovated building can be recognized as Hundertwasser's work, with its façade of bumpy and irregular black-and-white tile mosaics. This project also had trees as tenants, and Hundertwasser described it at the time of buildsing as "a piece of homeland, a piece of spontaneous vegetation in the anonymous and sterile city desert."

The use of living trees has become a recurring theme for many artists. Perhaps this is because, in Hundertwasser's words, as "representatives of the forest" they best symbolize ecological and social issues. Trees provide the earth with its longest-living and tallest life form. The American artist Vito Acconci has frequently used trees in his outdoor structures and projects. His "High Rise of Trees" for the Olympic Games in Atlanta in 1996 was a stack of four container-grown trees, one on top of the other, supported in a tall steel tower. His idea is to present living plants in striking, unusual contexts and dynamic spatial relationships. In the same year, at the Centro Gallego de Arte Contemporáneo, in Santiago de Compostela, Spain, Acconci extended this concept beyond the format of free-standing public sculpture into a more environmental work. "Park up a Building" called for the temporary installation of a public walk-in and sit-in "tree-scape" on one of the walls of the arts centre. The plain, stone-clad wall

FONDATION CARTIER BUILDING, PARIS, FRANCE
ARCHITECT: **JEAN NOUVEL**

▲ To preserve a group of established trees, Nouvel incorporated them into the front of the building as a sound-absorbing screen. The front and rear walls extend beyond the main body of the building, as seen in this side elevation, and are designed to embrace additional trees and landscaping.

FONDATION CARTIER BUILDING, PARIS, FRANCE
DESIGNER: **PATRICK BLANC**

▶ Framed like a picture by the steel structure of the building, Blanc's vertical garden was created by inserting young plants into pockets made into a type of plant propagation material. This curtain-like construction was then suspended outside a floor-to-ceiling window above the main entrance.

**SEA HAWK HOTEL AND
RESORT, FUKUOKA, JAPAN**
ARCHITECTS: **BALMORI
ASSOCIATES AND CESAR
PELLI ASSOCIATES**
LANDSCAPE ARCHITECTS:
**SOMA LANDSCAPE
PLANNING CO., LTD**

▼ The most inventive
features of this landscape
include wave-like sheets of
glass, four storeys high, down
which water slithers into a
canal below. One of the
sheets can seen on the left.

overlooked an uninspiring car park. The tree "park" was suspended from the roof of the three-storey building by aluminium bars, steel rods, and cables. These could be adjusted to suit other façades, making the "garden" portable and reusable. At the site in Santiago de Compostela they were secured so as to provide a series of rising, stepped platforms complete with "park benches." Individual trees, growing in linen bags and clamped between two horizontal metal grilles, provided the living element in this modern version of the hanging garden.

Vertical landscape features are also in evidence in a more conventional interiorscape at the Sea Hawk

Hotel and Resort, in Fukuoka, Japan. Designed by the consortium of Balmori Associates, Cesar Pelli Associates, and Soma Landscape Planning Co, Ltd, and completed in 1997, the complex has as its central feature an enclosed, covered garden. A large, arching roof of steel and glass spans a floor space given over almost entirely to a landscape of rockeries, water features, and lush planting, including large palms and ferns. The glasshouse, with its planted content, is not at all exceptional – a sort of modern-day Victorian palm house. What is different and noteworthy is the way in which the landscaping has been continued up the polychromatic façade of the adjoining Sea Hawk

Hotel, which forms one side of the covered garden. At ground level, a narrow canal runs the full length of the hotel wall and separates it from the landscaped glasshouse. Access to the accommodation and bars is provided by a number of bridges. The wall itself is planted by using long, horizontal troughs above the windows on every floor level. Most dramatic and eye-catching, however, are the waterfalls that cascade down the wall. Suspended in stainless-steel wire cradles that descend the full four-storey height of the wall are wavy panels of clear glass, 1m (3ft) wide. These transparent, ribbon-like panels resemble a series of rivers as water, pumped up from the canal at ground level, runs down them. The water lightly adheres to the glass through surface tension before flowing back into the canal.

Acconci's "Park up a Building" and the Sea Hawk Hotel's "water wall" both depend on the wall as the background for an imaginative planted environment. The Frenchman Patrick Blanc also works creatively with walls, making walls as gardens and gardens as walls. Blanc is a scientist, a professor of botany and a member of the highly respected Centre National de la Recherche Scientifique, yet it was the garden he created at the Chaumont International Festival of the Garden in France in 1994 that brought him to the attention of a wider audience. His contribution, "Murs Végétaux" (Vegetal Walls), took the form of a tall, free-standing, and slightly inclined wall that was covered on both sides with familiar garden plants. Instead of being viewed from above, as happens in the conventional garden, the living plants here were presented at a right angle to the ground. The wall stood in a rectangular pool of water from which the plants took nourishment hydroponically. In this method of cultivation plants are grown in a synthetic medium and fed by a water-based solution that contains all their necessary nutrients.

It was the possibilities suggested by Blanc's economic use of ground space that really caught the imagination. When floor space is restricted, why not grow upwards? The garden space in the urban environment is often limited, and if walls could be transformed into gardens, this could increase the opportunities for city dwellers to grow plants. This in

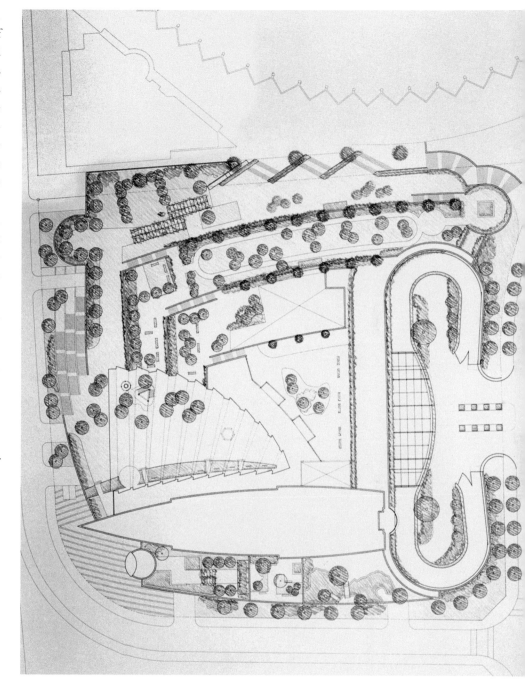

▲ A coloured plan of the Sea Hawk Hotel and Resort reveals that landscaping plays a substantial role in the design, both outside and inside the buildings. The central feature of the scheme, seen on the right, is a modern variation on the Victorian palm house, or winter garden. Here, beneath a curved roof of glass and steel, is a forest of exotic plants and a series of waterfalls that slowly descend the whole height of the building and replenish a canal below.

FOREST BUILDING, RICHMOND, VIRGINIA, USA
ARCHITECTS: **SITE**

◀ A view through the cleverly simulated breach in this brick wall shows one of several elevated walkways that connect the glass doors of the building's false front to the body of the store. The walkway takes shoppers above and through a jungle of oaks, shrubs, and ground cover.

▶ The wall on the Forest Building, seemingly torn apart by trees growing behind it, is just one of the eye-catching store frontages designed by the architectural group SITE for BEST Products in the USA. This one is a witty comment on what might happen when we encroach upon nature.

turn, could lead to a proliferation of green spaces in our environmentally unbalanced urban centres.

As a result of his success at Chaumont, Blanc was invited in 1998 to create a vertical garden to coincide with an exhibition on art and nature at the Fondation Cartier in Paris. The Cartier building is a modern, steel-framed structure with glass walls, and the vertical surface to be planted was also made of glass. The completed garden, which was set above the main entrance, was flanked on all sides by the steel frame of the building, and from a distance it looked almost like a giant abstract painting. Wild and jungle-like, it contrasted dramatically with the geometry and precision engineering of the building, and in addition it formed a living link between a line of trees to the front of the building and the gardens to the rear.

The Fondation Cartier building was designed by the French architect Jean Nouvel and completed in 1994. He decided to make use of a wall to embrace, rather than support, planting. He set the main part of

the building back from an avenue of cedar trees, as this allowed the trees, which were supplemented with additional ground-cover planting, to be retained. An outer, free-standing glass partition, the same height as the building, was then installed between the trees and the road. The tall glass screen and the trees form a barrier that is both real and psychological between the outside world and the Cartier galleries, where a peaceful, contemplative atmosphere is appropriate for the appreciation of works of art.

The idea of creating a planted barrier between a false façade and a building's outer wall is not unique to the Fondation Cartier project. In 1980 the New York-based architectural group SITE designed the Forest Building, a retail store in Richmond, Virginia, for BEST Products. What surprised shoppers on their first visit to the new store was the position of the front wall, which appeared to have been wrenched away from the rest of the building by the sudden emergence of a clump of trees.

Loosely associated with the Radical Architecture Movement of the 1970s, SITE's work is a fusion of art and architecture that often embraces landscape design and a concern for the environment. The group has created eight showrooms for BEST, whose approach to retailing meant that these display sites had to act as functional boxes. The architects managed to give each store a unique identity by the way in which they dealt with the main façade. At the Almeda-Genoa shopping centre, in Houston, Texas, the BEST store, built in 1975, looks like a crumbling ruin, while another of the company's stores the brick façade appears to be flaking away. SITE's unorthodox additions have made the opening of a BEST store an eagerly anticipated event, with the frontage of each new outlet being as memorable as the last.

The site chosen for the BEST store in Richmond was covered with trees and rich, varied vegetation. SITE's design aim was to respect the natural landscape, to preserve as much of it as possible in a way that would accentuate both the importance of showing consideration for the natural environment and the consequences of failure to do so. The dramatic front and main entrance of the building is designed to suggest that violated nature can fight back and sometimes win. The apparent intrusion of plant life into the store is achieved by splitting the building apart at the front. Towards the front of the store the side walls were constructed in such a way that they appear to have been severed and torn apart.

"RAINDROPS IN THE DUST," STRASBOURG, FRANCE
ARTIST: DOMINIQUE KIPPELEN

▲ An air vent above a disused storage chamber gives little clue as to what lies below. In the space beneath it Kippelen has created a subterranean garden, one of several that she has made in derelict warehouses in Strasbourg's port complex.

▶ Steps lead down to the dimly lit warehouse. Using discarded items and materials found in this and other abandoned multi-storey warehouses in the port area, the artist has made a secret garden – she has even managed to persuade grain to grow despite the limited amount of natural light. This is a garden as an artwork, an installation, intended to symbolize the resilience of nature and its ability to restore itself in the face of apparent destruction by the hand of man.

A jagged brick edge suggests that the façade has been forcibly separated from the rest of the building. Within the chasm between the fake wall and actual front of the building, giant oak trees and ground-cover shrubs have been allowed to grow and spread. To enter the store shoppers walk through and experience this "jungle." There is also an element of wit – unlike the Fondation Cartier building, this is a very ordinary structure, which seems simply to have been ripped apart by an apparently rampant and vengeful nature.

The façade of the BEST store in Richmond is more art than architecture. More art than landscape design is a fitting description of the "gardens" that the French artist Dominique Kippelen has attempted to make in abandoned underground chambers and derelict warehouses in Strasbourg, in France. Commercial traffic on the River Rhine has undergone a marked decline in recent years,

rendering many of this inland port's docks and warehouses redundant. However, some of the disused, run-down, multi-storey warehouses have been given new leases of life as indoor gardens.

Kippelen began creating her garden installations in Strasbourg in the mid-1990s. Her ideas were accepted with a degree of reluctance by the port authorities, but the main problem she faced in creating the gardens was not officialdom but the limited amount of natural light that enters the buildings. A garden that she created in 1995, to which she gave the evocative title "Raindrops in the Dust," is representative of her design process. She began by establishing a three-dimensional "floor-scape," which consisted of a series of mounds made from inorganic waste material that she found on the site. The remains of corrugated panels, discarded hollow concrete blocks, and other found objects and structures were

DUISBURG NORD LANDSCAPE PARK, DUISBURG, GERMANY

LANDSCAPE ARCHITECTS: **LATZ AND PARTNER**

▲ This view from a raised walkway looks down into the gardens created in the old coke and iron-ore bunkers at the former A.G. Thyssen steelworks. Each bunker has been turned into an individually designed walled garden. During reclamation of the site 240 plant species were found growing naturally in the bunkers; many had come from other countries, imported inadvertently with the iron ore.

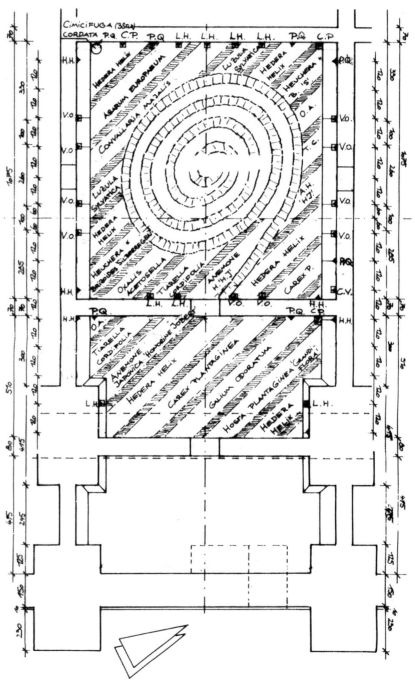

▲ One of the most interesting of the gardens is this simple but elegant design. A low wall of logs defines a spiral, gaining height as it runs outwards. Between the coils of the spiral is a series of planted beds.

▶ The plan shows the planting pattern used in the garden. Instead of following the spiral, the designer introduced bands of different plants – all ground-cover types – that cut across it diagonally.

then added to the scene. Surfaces that were exposed to light would eventually develop a covering of moss. Finally Kippelen spread on the floor a rich growing medium, in which she sowed grain. The grain sprouted even in the darker recesses of the warehouse, but only in the upper areas, where it received natural light, did it turn green. The green carpets thus formed take on an eerie appearance in the bands of light that creep through openings and roof lights. Kippelen's gardens have attracted many visitors, which has caused the authorities to have second thoughts about allowing access to the derelict buildings.

Such reluctance to encourage the use of a disused industrial site was not, fortunately, the attitude taken by the German city of Duisburg when it was deciding what should be done with the closed and disintegrating A.G. Thyssen steelworks. In 1989 the city authorities decided to make the area into a public park. An international competition was held and this was won by the designers Professor Peter Latz and Anna-Liese Latz. The 200-hectare (500-acre) Duisburg Nord Landscape Park is a long-term venture, but in 1994 it was sufficiently complete to be opened to the public. The project is committed to abiding by ecological principles, and high on the list of priorities of the team led by the Latzs is recycling. So far this has included the re-use of on-site materials, such as coal ore and even metal, to promote plant growth in the newly created gardens.

These gardens occupy the old coke and iron-ore bunkers and are visible from a raised metal walkway that was once an overhead railway. The individually designed "demonstration" gardens are contained within walls, but, unlike the traditional walled garden, the spaces formerly served as stores for the coke and ore needed to manufacture steel. Some of the gardens are almost inaccessible, and have been deliberately left so. They are designed to be looked at rather than to be occupied – a place where plants can become established and grow unhindered. Even the derelict walls are disappearing behind curtains of planting as climbing plants take hold. The old high walls restrict the amount of sunlight available, so shade-tolerant plants such as ferns, ivy, mosses, and hydrangeas have become established best.

DAWNRIDGE, BEVERLY HILLS, LOS ANGELES, USA
DESIGNER: **TONY DUQUETTE**

▲ In a remarkable project that takes the architectural folly to an extreme, tightly packed, plant-covered wooden buildings form a shanty town. Here, like sentries on guard, carved oriental figures line one of the many passageways.

▶ Many of the buildings are of ornate design and display a mixture of Western and Eastern influences. Each of them has become a spectacular garden whose every surface is given over to an array of pots of various shapes and sizes containing plants that are encouraged to scramble up walls and across roofs. This is a container garden conceived on a grand scale. and like other container gardens, it has the great advantage over a conventionally planted garden that it can be given a new look almost as easily as one might rearrange potted plants in the home.

The plants in these outdoor interiorscapes are growing in the ground, wheras in most commercial premises living vegetation inside or on the building grown in purpose-built or large, free-standing containers or planters. Often the plants are sustained by methods that do not require use of the ground, such as hydroponics. In the domestic environment, ceramic pots and hanging baskets, arranged casually about the home, tend to be the equivalent favoured solution. In most instances the enthusiastic efforts of private homeowners would not be regarded as contributions to interiorscapes.

An exception is an ongoing project by the interior designer Tony Duquette. On his land in Beverly Hills, California, he has created a verdant village that he has named Dawnridge. Wooden buildings adorned with hundreds of potted plants are clustered among a group of eucalyptus trees behind his house. These buildings, some on stilts above a stream, are based on a style seen widely in Thailand and Indonesia. Colourful, highly decorative, and packed together tightly, they envelop the original trees, which grow within and through them. But it is the pot plants above all that catch the eye. No surface, horizontal or vertical, is left free of vegetation. There are succulents and yuccas in ceramic pots on the wooden floors, staircases, and roofs, while others are perched precariously on wooden posts and balustrades. Spider plants grow from one pot to another, adding to this containerized jungle.

The artist and designer Hundertwasser (*pages 70–2*) was also obsessed with giving buildings and architecture over to plants. Unlike many of his contemporaries, however, he did not always see the need for conventional planters. To him, a sealed-off room with a window was a perfectly suitable home for a tree.

The Hundertwasser House, which he designed with the architect Peter Pelikan, was begun in 1977 in Vienna and the first residents moved in nine years later. As early as 1980 Hundertwasser had outlined the aims of the building and proclaimed an "obligation" to the tree, as it signified a "restoration of a dialogue with nature. An everyday life without intimate contact with trees, plants, soil and humus is unworthy of man." For him, this project was not a

THE HUNDERTWASSER HOUSE, VIENNA, AUSTRIA

ARTIST/DESIGNER: **HUNDERTWASSER**

ARCHITECT: **PETER PELIKAN**

▶ Many of Hundertwasser's architectural projects involved the renovation of existing buildings, but this apartment block was a new development. Its most striking feature is the forest that seems to have sprung up on the rooftop terraces. In fact, plants occupy nearly every available horizontal surface of the building, and some even emerge from windows. The artist's extraordinary green architecture has returned to nature a small corner of an otherwise plantless city environment.

matter of "putting approved plants in ever greater numbers in approved vases, buckets and tubs everywhere like decorative pieces of furniture. It is about helping nature grow wild in the city."

The implication of this philosophy for the design of the building was that trees, shrubs, ivy, and other climbers were considered to have just as much importance as the bricks and mortar. Hundertwasser's guiding principle was that all horizontal surfaces should belong to nature, with grass and trees allowed to occupy every available space. The numerous terraces and balconies, from the first floor upwards, are filled with soil up to 1m (3ft) deep, almost up to window level. All the "green surfaces" are accessible to the present residents, but Hundertwasser stipulated that the growth of plants and trees should "proceed as naturally as possible," without the interference of amateur gardeners.

The building, with its use of a multiplicity of materials, its different-sized, personalized windows, and its apparently random spatial organization, is architecture of an almost childlike expression, seemingly free of constraint. Yet this is a complex, three-dimensional form, designed to provide the many horizontal surfaces needed for the trees and shrubs. It is as much a multi-level wildlife garden as an apartment block, with plants and humans sharing the same space. In Hundertwasser's words, it is "an oasis of humanity and nature."

Modern materials make it relatively easy to establish plants in architectural spaces such as floors and terraces. When the challenge involves a ceiling, however, a different strategy is required. The American designer and artist Martha Schwartz had to resort to artificial flowers for her redesign of an

SHEATS, LOS ANGELES, USA
ARCHITECT: **JOHN LAUTNER**

▶ This view of the entrance area of the house shows a trapezoidal pool that is fed by a low waterfall. The living room, on the far side of the pool, is reached by crossing stepping stones made of glass and concrete. After dark, ingeniously designed lighting renders the glass wall of the living room invisible. This has the attractive effect of making the external landscaping and the pool appear to be extensions of the internal living space.

uninviting new terminal at the Robert Mueller Municipal Airport in Austin, Texas. Space on the floor and walls was limited, mainly because of the volume of travellers, so the only available area was the ceiling.

When Austin wanted to expand and improve the airport, Schwartz was one of a number of artists commissioned to create site-specific works for the 24-hectare (59-acres) site. Completed in 1998, her "Hanging Texas Bluebonnet Field" was the only one created indoors. The Texas bluebonnet is the state flower, and Schwartz acquired hundreds of silk imitations, which she hung upside down on chains from the ceiling of the terminal. The suspended flowers, arranged in straight lines, stretch from the main doors to the single concourse, hiding a drab,

concrete, barrel-vaulted ceiling. Hanging about 1m (3ft) above travellers' heads, they swayed in the draughts caused by the opening and closing of the automatic doors. For arriving travellers the work provide an unusual floral welcome to Texas.

Throughout the centuries plants have played an important role in landscape and garden design, and so has water. In the design of many gardens water is more important than the planting. This is true of the late-Renaissance garden at the Villa d'Este, at Tivoli, near Rome, where great fountains, waterfalls, and cascades dominate the hillside site. Today, many domestic gardens have ponds or other ornamental water features. Water is also a component of gardens and landscapes within buildings.

ARANGO, ACAPULCO BAY, MEXICO

ARCHITECT: JOHN LAUTNER

◀ At the rear of the house the elevated terrace and moat follow the shape and profile of the exposed hillside. The existing sloping terrain was adopted as part of the architectural scheme, and, after some additional planting and landscaping, provided the house with an informal rock garden.

▶ Perched on the side of a hill overlooking the bay, the terrace serves as an outdoor living and dining area. Like a modern version of the ha-ha, the moat allows the terrace to connect visually with the surrounding seascape. In this way the curves of the terrace and the moat echo the distant coastline.

The American architect John Lautner frequently employed pools and waterfalls as an integral part of his schemes for private residences. Lautner, who died in 1994, established a reputation for his designs for multi-level private residences on sloping sites. He had been influenced by Frank Lloyd Wright, for whom he had worked as an apprentice at the Taliesin School. He also worked for Wright during the building of Fallingwater, Pennsylvania, a house designed by Wright and celebrated for its sympathetic relationship to its surroundings.

Many of Lautner's solutions required the house to be built projecting above the ground. In such instances outdoor living space, landscaping, and even driveways often had to be included within the structure of the building. Beyond the confines of the architecture, the remainder of the site – usually an exposed hillside – was untouched and left to nature. This is the case at Sheats, a private house in Los Angeles. Designed by Lautner in 1963 and remodelled in 1989, the building in plan resembles an angular hourglass and consists largely of a vast platform that projects out from the hillside. The main, external entrance to the living room is reached by crossing a series of geometric stepping stones that span a formal pond into which water cascades over a low wall. The water extends to the glass walls of the living room on two sides, and, when the glass doors are open, the "entrance pool" becomes an extension of the interior space.

One of Lautner's most celebrated private houses, Arango, completed in 1973, sits on a steep hill above Acapulco Bay, Mexico. Curvilinear rather than angular, the living area projects out beyond the bedrooms and service areas below. The most striking feature is the terrace, a curved concrete slab that sweeps out into space towards the bay. On the terrace a water-filled moat meanders around a central outdoor living and dining area to which two gently arched bridges give access. The moat keeps out crawling insects and does away with the need for railings or a balustrade. In the absence of any obvious barriers, the water-edged terrace appears to merge with the seascape below. A vast, semicircular concrete canopy sweeps over the terrace to provide shelter and shade, while other concrete projections form planted terraces.

A water garden in the form of a roof is the central feature of a temple designed by the Japanese architect Tadao Ando. Hompukuji temple, at Tsuna-gun, in Hyogo Prefecture, was completed in 1991 and sits on a rise on an island overlooking Osaka Bay. The new main hall of this temple used by the Buddhist Shingon sect is set into the ground immediately below a large, oval pool decorated with aquatic lotus plants that float on the surface of the water. For Buddhists water is the first element of creation and they further believe that water gave birth to the lotus flower, the symbol of the spiritual awakening of the Buddha. The water garden is the last obstacle in a complex journey that helps monks cast off everyday concerns and prepare the mind for contemplation.

To gain access to the prayer room devotees must descend a narrow flight of steps set between two parallel walls that divide the pool. The water garden has two architectural functions, acting as both an entrance to, and a roof for, the prayer room below.

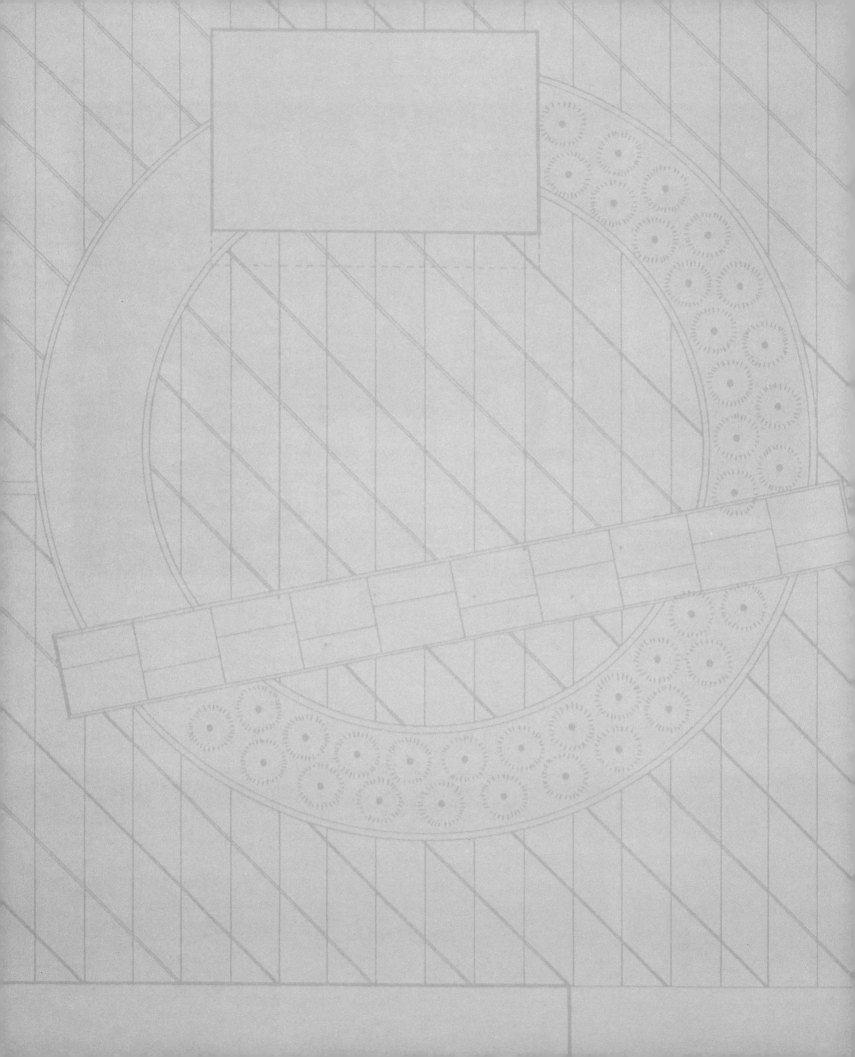

multi-storey gardens ▶

Skyscrapers were first built in Chicago towards the end of the nineteenth century. They relied upon internal fireproofed steel skeletons that supported the floors and internal partitions, replacing the external supporting walls. The invention of this steel-frame method of construction allowed the erection of tall buildings in which the outer wall was simply a facing, or "curtain wall," and this could even be made of glass. Since then the skyscraper has become the solution for inner-city housing and car parking, as well as a symbol of corporate power. With the continuing need to build upwards, it is not surprising that landscape design and gardens have become part of the multi-storey phenomenon. One of the most impressive landscape schemes to be incorporated in to a high-rise building is that which forms an integral and essential part of the Commerzbank headquarters in Frankfurt, Germany. The 298m (978ft), sixty-storey building designed by the British architectural practice of Foster and Partners was completed in 1997.

In plan the tower is a slightly rounded equilateral triangle. The corners contain the services, lifts, and staircases, while the sides, which are 60m (197ft) long, incorporate the offices. These surround a triangular central atrium, which acts as a ventilation chimney. To allow as much light as possible into the core of the building and to improve air circulation, the tower's glass-walled office accommodation is interrupted every eight storeys by a four-storey winter garden.

The gardens are arranged in a spiral-like series around the three-sided tower, which means that, on any given floor of the tower, two sides are occupied by offices while the other one forms part of the multi-storey winter garden. In other words, in a plan

COMMERZBANK HEADQUARTERS, FRANKFURT, GERMANY
ARCHITECTS: **FOSTER AND PARTNERS**

▶ The ingenious design of the three-sided tower allows occupants to look on to one of the series of internal, four-storey winter gardens.

▲ The roof garden is seen
here from one of the
surrounding tall office
buildings. Kept moist
by water jets, the granite
circle acts like a mirror to
reflect the sky and the
bamboos. The diamond
shape of the paving slabs
creates an illusion: they
look like rectangular slabs
seen obliquely and the
floor appears to tilt at
a strange angle.

of a typical floor, only two sides of the triangular
building are occupied by offices. This ingenious
arrangement enables all the inward-facing offices
in the building to receive natural sunlight and
provides the staff with pleasant views of a garden. The
spiral configuration of the architectural space is
similar to the way in which nature arranges the leaves
about the stem of a young plant. Imitating nature, the
architects aimed in this way to maximize the natural
light reaching both offices and gardens.

A slightly recessed glass wall protects the gardens
from the outside world. Internally, the gardens open
on to the central atrium, separated only by a raised
planting bed. In plan, the design of the winter gardens
– all of which are identical – echoes the triangular
theme of the building. A triangular raised planting
area, containing trees and shrubs, sits either side of a

central triangular terrace, one side of which faces on
to the central atrium. The terrace includes permanent
seating and is linked to the offices either side of the
garden by a pathway that bisects the raised planted
areas. Entered under a canopy of vegetation, the
gardens provide staff with their own "local" garden
in which to relax and take lunch. The building is, in
effect, a series of "villages" stacked one on top of the
other, each with its own landscaped garden.

The Commerzbank's gardens could also be seen
as a series of indoor roof gardens, since each is located
above an eight-storey block of offices. Roof gardens
are usually found at the top of buildings, but at the
YKK Research and Development Centre in Tokyo,
Japan, a roof garden has been created inside and near
the base of a multi-storey development. It is located in
an elevated courtyard surrounded by high-rise

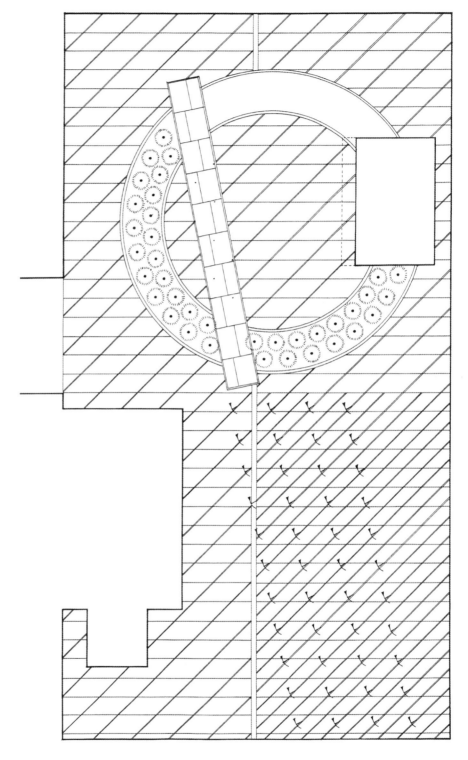

offices. The courtyard has an area of approximately 650 sq m (7000 sq ft) and, in addition to the adjacent office space, is flanked by an exhibition hall, a cafe, and a hotel. This roof garden, designed by Toru Mitani and completed in 1993, is unusual in that it can be viewed from the offices above.

Mitani has created a bold, simple, geometric design that takes advantage of the fact that the garden will be seen mainly from overhead. The overall plan consists of a circle inscribed within a rectangle, with the main visual interest provided by the treatment of these clearly defined floor spaces. The circular area, the central feature of the garden, is made of slabs of black granite in a delicately defined grid pattern. The surface of the granite floor is kept moist and made highly reflective by a watery mist sprayed by lines of sprinklers that cut across the circle. The dark wet granite acts like a mirror, reflecting the surrounding building, as well as the sky and passing clouds. Numerous rainbows are formed when sunlight is refracted through the jets of mist.

The circle of granite is surrounded by a precisely cut grassy mound, a rooftop earthwork, on top of which is a planted a ring of tall bamboos. These plants sway in the breezes that funnel through gaps between the closely spaced buildings enclosing the courtyard space. What appears to be a walkway, made from a series of steel grilles, cuts across the mound and the granite circle. This pathway is only for those brave enough to venture among the water sprays.

The remaining rectangular rooftop space is paved in a pattern designed to read differently from various

ATLANTIS APARTMENT BUILDING, MIAMI, USA

ARCHITECTS:
ARQUITECTONICA

◀ The blue grid framing pairs of balconies also defines a square hole that pierces the building. Red and yellow elements highlight the open-air space, while a single palm tree suggests that it might be a garden – if a rather unconventional one.

▶ In this view from the top of the red spiral staircase, the strong curving lines of the white railings, the yellow wall, and the kidney-shaped swimming pool combine to create an organic space that contrasts boldly with the straight exterior lines of the building. The palm tree adds to this contrast, as well as providing the pool with welcome shade.

angles. What appears as a diamond pattern when viewed from above looks like a chequerboard when seen from eye or ground level. This optical illusion helps to animate the space, which is further enlivened by a kinetic sculpture. The client's brief required a sculptural feature to be located outside the company's boardroom, which also overlooks the courtyard. Instead of installing a single object, Mitani opted for a multi-element floor-based sculpture. Forty small red mobiles are arranged in a diagonal formation that occupies one quarter of the space. Described as "wind fish," they "swim" in the currents of air, making visible the effects of drafts and breezes that would otherwise go unnoticed. In this way they act like weathervanes and, along with the swaying bamboo and the "sky mirror" of wet granite, they provide office workers using the garden with a simple and up-to-the-minute guide to the local weather.

Mitani's design represents a break from the traditional Japanese approach to landscape design, which relied on symbolism or storytelling. This roof garden is not based on any historical formula but has instead been designed as a response to the prevailing weather conditions, affecting the building and its occupants. In addition, the designer has chosen to use modern high-tech materials instead of the natural elements associated with the traditional Japanese garden, to create a rooftop landscape that changes with the wind and sky.

An outdoor space spectacularly exposed to the elements can be found in the Atlantis apartment building at Biscayne Bay, Miami, Florida, designed by Arquitectonica and completed in 1982. When a communal landscaped space is incorporated within a residential or commercial building it is usually as a glazed winter garden, an enclosed courtyard, or a roof garden. However, in the Atlantis building the "garden" space is simply a vast, four-storey, square hole punched through the middle of the eighteen-storey building. Primary shapes and colours provide the "decorative" features of the building, which is essentially a slender, rectangular box. One of the two long elevations is a sheer wall of glass, while the other, the south-facing side, contains the apartments' balconies, which are arranged within a bold blue grid. Connecting these two principal elevations of the building is the square void of the leisure garden.

The garden is bordered on one side by a curving yellow wall punctuated by an entrance door and the balcony and patio doors of an adjacent apartment. A bright-red spiral staircase provides access from the apartments on the other side. A terrace, with a kidney-shaped swimming pool and a single palm tree, affords spectacular views of the Florida landscape. The Atlantis apartments display one of the most unusual relationships between building and exterior garden space, and this relationship provides the façade of the building with its most striking architectural feature. The solitary palm tree, completely out of context, adds an element of wit to this.

The Atlantis apartments and the Commerzbank headquarters building represent the diversity that has marked the evolution of the multi-storey garden. Such gardens were first introduced in the early 1960s, with the introduction of the atrium as an architectural feature in many tall buildings. In North America, among the first buildings with a large atrium were the Hyatt Regency hotels, designed by the architect John Portman. In each hotel the rooms are arranged around a glazed, multi-storey atrium distinguished by trailing plants that descend in cascades from the balconies overlooking the central space.

Portman, who is also a painter and sculptor, began in architectural practice in 1953. He has established a reputation for innovative solutions for urban architecture owing to his desire to create built environments, both private and public, that enhance the quality of life. He has achieved this by integrating

HYATT REGENCY HOTEL, ATLANTA, USA

ARCHITECT: **JOHN PORTMAN**

▶ This futuristic hotel atrium has been frowned upon as "glitzy," but the architect has certainly made good use of vegetation. Plants cascade from every floor to make this towering space a highly theatrical indoor garden.

architecture with nature. It was the design for his first major hotel, the Hyatt Regency in Atlanta, that originally attracted interest in his work and played a part in revolutionizing subsequent hotel design.

Other Hyatt Regency hotels, designed by Portman and following the design established in Atlanta, can be seen in Baltimore and San Francisco. The gilt-finish decorative details, the elaborate, abstract sculptural structures, and the sparkling lighting combine to bring to mind a Baroque cathedral. The overwhelming sense of luxury is exemplified by the glass cubicles of the atrium lifts, which, like ornate historic carriages, transport residents to the floors above. Such ostentatious design has offended many architectural critics, but this need not blind us to Portman's clever use of planting. *Philodendron scandens* tumbles from every balcony of every floor, transforming the atrium into a spectacular indoor hanging garden.

One of the most celebrated of the early multi-storey atrium gardens belongs to the Ford Foundation Building in New York – a project completed in 1969. The architects were Kevin Roche and John Dinkeloo, who gave responsibility for the interior atrium garden to the young landscape architect Dan Kiley. As a student Kiley had been inspired by the work of the Bauhaus, the German school of architecture and applied design founded in 1919 by the architect Walter Gropius. Kiley came into contact with the philosophy of the Bauhaus at the Harvard Graduate School of Design, where Gropius, who had fled Nazi Germany, taught architecture. Kiley was studying landscape design but attended the architect's lectures and was impressed by the Bauhaus principles of standardization and rationalization, which meant a rejection of ornamentation in favour of forms determined by function.

Dan Kiley is now one of America's most respected landscape designers, with a style that combines the formality of the French seventeenth-century garden and contemporary rational thinking. In the 1960s his understanding of and feeling for modernism and contemporary architecture made him an ideal candidate to design the Ford Foundation Building's interior landscaping. In doing so he created one of the first, and certainly the most significant, of the

multi-storey gardens that have become familiar features of office buildings and hotels.

The glazed garden is protected by the glass walls and roof of the twelve-storey building's south-east corner and is overlooked internally by twelve storeys of glazed office space. The garden is at ground level, and because the building sits on a sloping site, the design of the garden had to cope with a change in level of 4m (13ft). Kiley introduced staircases and pathways to lead through the garden and to break it up into a series of rectilinear planting areas. These are planted with trees, supplemented with ground cover and foliage shrubs. The space was originally planted with large examples of *Ficus benjamina* and *Magnolia grandiflora*, but because the latter did not adapt and failed to become established, the whole of the planting scheme has recently been renovated.

FORD FOUNDATION BUILDING, NEW YORK CITY, USA
LANDSCAPE ARCHITECT: **DAN KILEY**
ARCHITECTS: **ROCHE AND DINKELOO**

▶ The unstructured planting of ground cover, mixed evergreen shrubs, and trees, rising in a series of banks, conceals the rigidity of Kiley's geometric and formal ground plan.

▼ A cross-sectional drawing shows how the landscaping rises up through the building in a series of planted terraces.

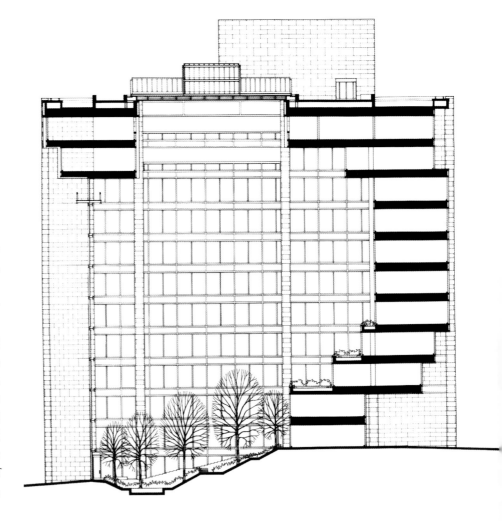

A formal pool adds further interest and provided an opportunity to introduce marginal and aquatic plants. The garden continues upwards, ascending the atrium in a series of stepped terraces until it reaches the fifth floor, and plants also hang from containers set high up on the eleventh floor.

Much more compact than this at only two storeys high, the courtyard garden in the Powerlink Queensland Headquarters Building, in Brisbane, Australia, completed in 1997, illustrates the lasting popularity of the fully enclosed, air-conditioned interior garden. Here, unlike the Ford Foundation Building, the landscaped courtyard is surrounded by open-plan offices. Staircases lead up from the courtyard to offices that have no glazed partitions but instead open directly on to planted balconies. The style of the landscaping is also very different from Kiley's restrained, geometric formalism. Here, the scheme, designed by the architects Peddle Thorp, is intended to contrast with the functional architecture of the surrounding office complex; and the rectilinear floor space is given over to an elaborate organic composition. The planting is contained within curvilinear, asymmetrical islands, which are defined by sweeping paths that connect the building's entrances to ground-floor rooms and staircases. Extending from a circular lily pond outside the boardroom, a watercourse passes beneath paths as it meanders across the garden to further define areas of planting. Stepping stones provide additional crossing points, and rocks contribute to the naturalistic look of the design. The dense planting of subtropical foliage plants, such as palms, ferns, weeping figs, and bromeliads, is used to create secluded sitting areas that

POWERLINK QUEENSLAND HEADQUARTERS BUILDING, BRISBANE, AUSTRALIA
ARCHITECTS: **PEDDLE THORP**

◄ Usually, planting in an office building is confined to free-standing planters. Here, palms and ferns are growing in a contoured landscape that is easily reached from the open-plan offices.

► This plan drawing reveals flowing, organic forms that create a sense of movement within the rectangular shape of the garden. Paths lead from external entrances to offices and stairs, while stepping stones provide the office workers with additional routes through the ground-floor space.

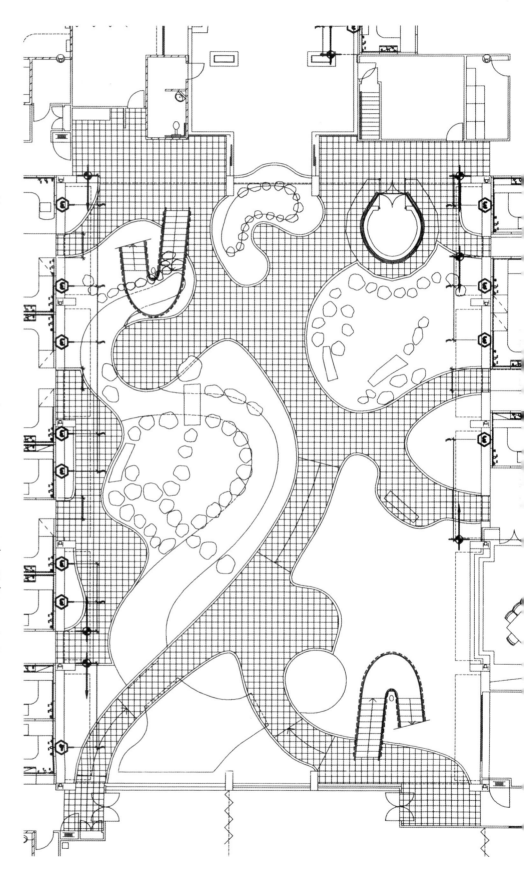

MERRILL LYNCH BUILDING, DENVER, USA

LANDSCAPE ARCHITECTS: **TVS&A**

◀ Subtle night-time lighting brings out the textural quality of this naturalistic interior landscape, which contrasts strongly with the linear emphasis of the surrounding architecture. A low-key waterfall and meandering stream add movement and sound.

McCORMICK CONVENTION CENTER EXPANSION, CHICAGO, USA

DESIGNER: **WET DESIGN**

▶ Although they look like solid rods, of stainless steel perhaps, the arching forms are in fact precisely controlled jets of water. In a further illusion, the water below them suggests a sheet of mirror glass.

are suitable for work or relaxation. At night the garden is lit by low-key light sources, including underwater spotlights and bollard-style path lights.

A garden spanning three levels in the main atrium of the Merrill Lynch Building in Denver, Colorado, indicates a similar desire to create a style of landscape that is the antithesis of the modernist architecture enclosing it. Although the architectural detailing of the building suggests a relaxed modernist style, the interior landscape, designed by TVS&A, is by contrast almost picturesque. Rough-cut stone walls define borders and landscape spaces, and form raised planters. From one section of wall, beside a pebble-lined pool and stream, water "weeps" over projecting stone blocks to create a gently flowing waterfall. Elsewhere, grassy banks, randomly placed rocks, and informal planting all contribute to this suggestion of a natural landscape.

The use of materials such as natural stone for the garden's walls suggests a romantic yearning for a man-made environment that has been hand-crafted and is on a human scale rather than anonymous and industrially manufactured. Whereas the villas of Renaissance Italy and the palaces of seventeenth-century France engendered a garden style that was in keeping with the spirit of the architectural language of the time, here, in this twentieth-century atrium, the landscape hints at a bygone era.

More sculptural and contemporary is the waterscape created by WET Design in 1997 for the McCormick Convention Center Expansion in Chicago. The building's enormous five-storey lobby features a water display rather than a planted landscape. A series of perfectly controlled, uninterrupted jets of water arc across raised channels of perfectly still, mirror-like water. Protected from

the elements by the glass walls of a building, water can be sculpted to achieve effects impossible in an exterior environment exposed to the weather. According to WET Design, the control of the water at the McCormick Convention Center is based on "axis-symmetric laminar flow." The science might be baffling but in this sheltered interior it has enabled the designers to sculpt water into precise forms and completely motionless surfaces. Fountains and water features have long been an essential part of garden history, with great gardens such as that at the Villa d'Este near Rome designed around them. WET Design's elegant solution shows that trees and shrubs are not always necessary to provide landscape interest within an interior space.

Both the McCormick Center and the atrium of the Merrill Lynch Building are modest spaces compared with the 67,500-sq m (727,000-sq ft) atrium and lobby of the Washington State Convention and Trade Center in Seattle. The building is essentially a multi-level bridge spanning twelve lanes of Interstate 5 in the city's downtown area. Designed by Danadjieva and Koenig Associates, and completed in 1992, the scheme for the atrium and lobby reflects Angela Danadjieva's belief that urban spaces must be multi-functional. Firstly, the three-storey space is designed to welcome and direct visitors to the conference facilities, retail outlets, and

WASHINGTON STATE CONVENTION AND TRADE CENTER, SEATTLE, USA
INTERIOR AND LANDSCAPE ARCHITECTS: **DANADJIEVA AND KOENIG ASSOCIATES**

▲ Looking up at the atrium's glass-panelled roof, between the overhanging concrete walls and cascading plants, is reminiscent of the view from the bottom of a canyon. The dynamic green landscape rises up from the floor to envelop the whole building.

▶ At night, in artificial light, the lobby is a complex and dramatic composition of angular concrete forms, with mysterious crevices inviting investigation. A strong impression of mass and weight is achieved by the subtle modulation of light and shade.

offices. Secondly, it is intended to provide the building with a series of interior plazas that can be used for public meetings and events.

The treatment of this quite extensive atrium and lobby is characterized by Danadjieva's inventive employment of concrete to shape the interior space. Using a combination of spray-on concrete, pre-cast panels, and poured concrete made on site, she sculpted the interior walls to create a Cubist-style surface resembling a rock face full of crevices and overhangs. The concrete walls are in fact intended to mimic the basalt formations of the north-western region of the USA. The highly textured surface of the cast concrete was created by using a deliberately uneven timber shuttering, and the forms themselves are hollow to reduce weight.

The angular concrete wall steps upward in a series of vertical and horizontal planes, which increasingly overhang as they reach the glazed panel roof; this allows a glimpse of the sky and provides the main source of natural light for this man-made chasm. Trees perch perilously on top of jutting concrete blocks, and additional planting is squeezed on to ledges from which trailing plants tumble and spill downwards over the concrete walls. In nature, plants adapt in order to grow in the most unlikely of locations, and here, as in a natural mountainous environment, the planting is below, beside and above you. It is a dynamic landscape, not a passive one.

The lower level of the building is dedicated to vehicle movement and to parking. The levels above ground are for use by pedestrians only, and here stairs and pathways lead through the concrete mountains, the dramatic effect of which is enhanced by spectacular waterfalls and abundant vegetation. The planting, which includes schefflera, philodendron, and ficus, produces a subtropical atmosphere. Danadjieva has created a three-dimensional landscape that is not so much a garden as an interior park in which architecture and landscape are fused.

By contrast, in some buildings the architecture and interior landscape design are not planned as an integrated whole. In such cases the landscape designer, who is often brought in towards the end of the architectural process, can be presented with a

space that proves very challenging, particularly if the requested solution involves planting.

This was the situation that faced landscape designers Michel Desvigne and Christine Dalnoky when asked to create an interior garden for the European Parliament in Strasbourg, France. The space allocated was a narrow interior passage that cut through the main body of the building. Flanked on both sides by offices, this "street," as it is known, is less than 7m (23ft) wide, but over 30m (130ft) high and 200m (660ft) long. Natural light enters through the glass roof of the "street," which is rather like a multi-storey, modern version of a nineteenth-century shopping arcade.

The tall, narrow space seems ideal for trees, which would eagerly grow upwards towards the glass roof to gain light. But Desvigne and Dalnoky thought that trees would be out of scale and would also distract from the visual appearance of the space, concealing the strong vertical lines of the architecture. There was also a practical reason – the tree canopies would restrict light to those offices on the lower levels.

The designers' solution for the scheme, which they completed in 1996, was to create a vertical wall garden using climbing plants. They decided on vines but rejected delicate, floral domestic species in favour of faster-growing invasive and tropical types with strong cords. The vines were supplemented with philodendrons, which also have lush foliage. Attracted by the light above, the vines have swiftly grown up the cables fixed to the roof of the building and in the process they complement the strong vertical lines of the architecture.

The plants are kept in good condition by small hoses that spray a fine mist on to their leaves imitating the moist tropical conditions preferred by the vines. Fibre-optic wires on either side of these climbing plants illuminate the vertical garden at night. *Fatsia japonica*, with its distinctive large, finger-like leaves, completes the planting at ground level.

There is one designer whose commissions are almost always concerned with improving an existing architectural environment. The Frenchman Patrick Blanc (*pages 75–7*) makes gardens on the walls of buildings. The wall garden he created in 2001 for Hôtel

EUROPEAN PARLIAMENT, STRASBOURG, FRANCE
LANDSCAPE ARCHITECTS: **MICHEL DESVIGNE AND CHRISTINE DALNOKY**
▶ Jungle-like vines, philodendrons, and monsteras rise up from the floor on wires, in search of the light above. It is an effective but ingeniously simple planting solution to a tall, narrow corridor. Rather than interrupting or concealing this challenging space, the regimented rows of climbing plants give the impression that it extends endlessly.

**HOTEL PERSHING HALL,
PARIS, FRANCE**
DESIGNER: **PATRICK BLANC**

◀ Blanc has turned a hotel's
six-storey courtyard wall
into a sculptural relief of
living plants. Arranged
in an apparently random
and natural-looking
composition, the plants
display a great variety
of texture and colour.
This living sculpture
was made possible by
modern technology and
the natural adaptability
of plants.

▶ The designer's plan reveals
the complexity of his
planting scheme. The
drawing looks similar to
a conventional planting
plan, but on this site the
"ground" is vertical and
the design has to allow
for the fact that the
plants, as they grow,
will turn upwards
towards the light.

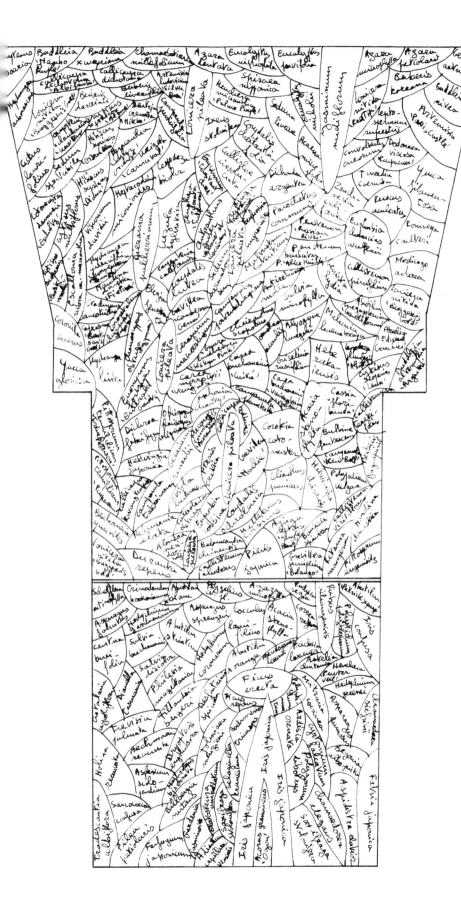

Pershing Hall in Paris is one of the more unusual variations on the theme of the multi-storey garden. The windowless courtyard wall, which rises up six floors, was transformed into a vertical garden by Blanc's specially designed out-of-ground growing system. The plants are inserted into pockets within a stiff, felt-like membrane just 13mm (½in) thick, and are sustained by a hydroponic system that drips nutrient-enriched water through the felt. The plants take root in the felt, strengthening the whole structure. This is Blanc's most ambitious project to date, and the 30m (100ft) high wall stretches the growing system to its limits.

Blanc's choice of plants is based on his research into the types that grow naturally in conditions that are both shady and have poor soil. Generally, he uses large foliage plants at the base of the vertical garden and smaller, more floriferous types towards the top, as this area of the garden gets more sun. He also makes use of plants that grow naturally with little or even no soil. There are two main types: epiphytes and lithophytes. Epiphytes are non-parasitic plants that use host plants for support but do not damage them; many have aerial roots to collect moisture from the air. Mosses, some orchids, and many bromeliads come into this category. Lithophytes, which include a number of orchids, are plants that will grow on stones or rock surfaces where there is little soil. More conventional garden plants, such as buddleia, spiraea, and ficus, have also proved successful in Blanc's vertical gardens.

This designer proves that by using modern growing methods and the right plants, one can create gardens in places and on surfaces generally considered unsuitable for vegetation. Ivy plants have long smothered and camouflaged buildings often several storeys high but in taking hold they can damage the integrity of the wall on which they depend for their support. Blanc's "vegetal walls" are separated from the wall of the building by a plastic membrane and in effect are no more than a surface dressing that clothes the architecture in plants. His multi-storey gardens provide an unorthodox but original way of introducing more plants into the urban environment. After all, when space on the ground is limited, why not follow the example of urban housing and grow vertically?

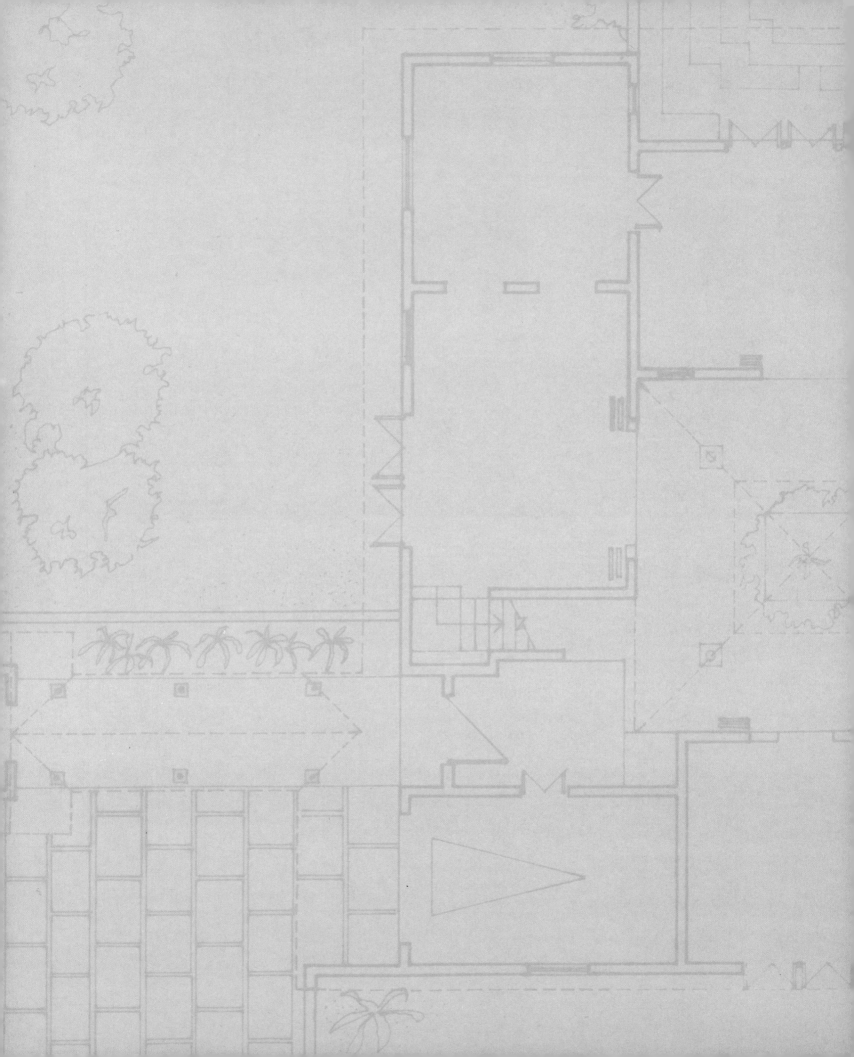

enclosed garden rooms ▶

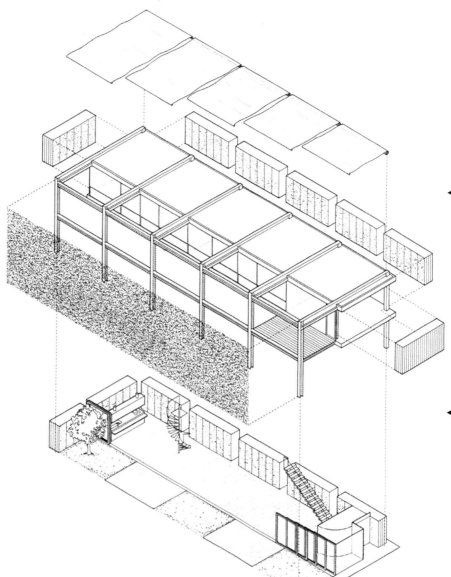

IVY STRUCTURE, SUGINAMI-
KU, TOKYO, JAPAN

ARCHITECT: **SHIGERU BAN**

◄ When the glass partitions
are drawn back, the
multi-purpose living
space on the ground floor
becomes as one with the
open-air garden courtyard.
The mass of ivy to the left
conceals an outer structural
frame. This living, two-
storey wall provides privacy
and acts as a soundproof
barrier yet still allows light
to penetrate.

◄ This isometric exploded
drawing reveals the
structure of the building.
Visible on the left is the
ivy-clad frame that supports
the steel beams from which
the first floor is suspended.
At the top of the drawing
are the fabric blinds that
can be extended over the
building to provide shade
and shelter.

The enclosed garden room is a contemporary interpretation of the traditional courtyard garden, which in turn had its origins in the development of the Roman villa. During the Roman Empire the concept of the courtyard garden evolved out of a necessity to make the best use of limited space in overcrowded and rapidly expanding cities. The solution was to put the garden within the house instead of around it.

There were two types of Roman garden: the large open gardens such as that created for Hadrian's Villa at Tivoli, near Rome, and enclosed gardens such as those created in urban environments including Pompeii. In the first type, the house was in the garden, in the second the architecture surrounded the garden, like a room without a roof. Small Italian houses such as those in Rome and Pompeii were built around an atria, consisting of central floored and roofed court with holes open to the sky in the centre to allow smoke to escape; sometimes there were ornamental ponds below the holes to collect rainwater. Beyond the atrium there was always another enclosed space, completely open to the sky; this was called the *hortus* and was for the production

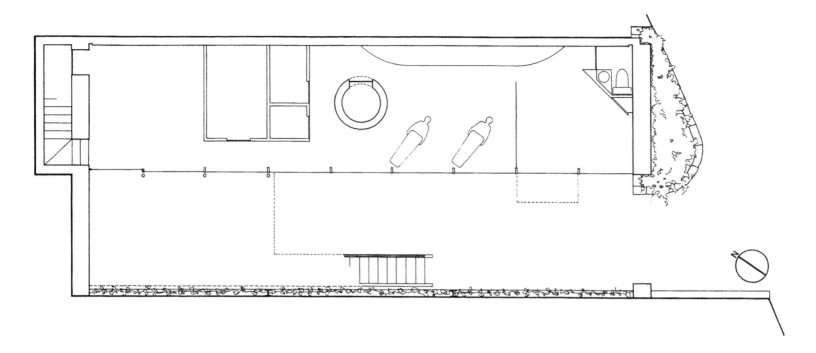

HOUSE FOR A DENTIST, SETAGAYA-KU, TOKYO, JAPAN

ARCHITECT: **SHIGERU BAN**

◄ To provide privacy for this house, which is squeezed into a narrow space between others, the architect has used quick-growing ivy to form a three-storey translucent screen. All the windows face this ivy barrier and have a view of a nearby cherry tree. The space on the left is for vehicles and also gives access to the dentist's surgery. The steps beyond lead to a private decked terrace and to the living quarters.

▲ The ground-floor plan of the surgery reveals that the building is divided longitudinally into two sections: an indoor space and an outdoor one. Only a transparent wall of glass separates the inside living space from the outside space.

of vegetables. It soon, however, became a pleasure garden as a greater proportion of Roman society enjoyed a wealthier lifestyle with more leisure time.

The traditional design of the Roman villa was thus modified to accommodate an internal garden. This new garden space was an integral part of the architectural framework of the house, taking the form of a courtyard open to the sky, surrounded on all sides by a covered walkway, or portico, with a colonnade. In the centre of the garden there was usually a pool and a fountain, recalling the earlier atrium, and the rest of the space was given over to lush planting criss-crossed by paths. Rooms opened on to this external enclosed space, which provided the house with natural light and ventilation, as well as allowing ease of movement between rooms.

Japan also has a history of gardens within buildings, and this continues today in the houses built in the traditional style in Kyoto. The small raked gravel-and-stone Zen garden contained within the wooden architecture of the house is intended to symbolize the natural landscape and thus enable its spirit to be brought inside the house. It is this tradition, rather than that of the Roman courtyard garden, that has inspired the architect Shigeru Ban, whose designs for domestic houses give equal importance to interior and exterior space.

Ivy Structure, a house completed in 1998 in the Tokyo suburb of Suginami-Ku typifies Ban's approach. Squeezed in between other, older properties, it occupies a long, narrow piece of land that runs from east to west. Privacy from adjoining houses was an essential requirement, but the architect's aim was to maximize the restricted site and to give the clients – a family of five – a sense of open space rather than confinement.

Ban's solution is a dwelling that includes both an outer architectural space and a more private interior one. The private section contains a spacious multi-purpose living area on the ground floor and four rooms and two bathrooms on the first floor. Sliding glass panels allow the ground-floor living space to be opened along its entire length on to the outer private courtyard. The uninterrupted flow of space from inside to outside is achieved by Ban's ingenious use of the building's southern wall, which is a two-storey, twin-layered, ivy-clad screen separating the house from the neighbouring property. The ivy cleverly disguises the structural function of this outer wall, which serves to support the steel girders from which the first floor is suspended. Hanging the first floor in this way dispenses with the need for supporting members or posts between the ground-floor living area and the outside space. The result is a single, large,

continuous space with no division between house and garden. Sliding fabric canopies can be extended along the upper steel girders to provide shelter and shade for the courtyard garden below. Ban fuses architecture with garden, and the important southern supporting wall is also a living planted feature. The courtyard garden, with its lawns, paved sitting areas, and single tree, which can all be covered by a canopy when required, is an unambiguous expression of the modern concept of the outside room.

A house for a dentist by the same architect, situated in the Tokyo suburb of Setagaya-Ku and completed in 1994, also required a solution for a long, rectangular site. Ban's answer, as with his Ivy Structure, was to divide the space in half lengthwise, making one side an open, exterior space and the other an interior space in which the living quarters (first and second floors) and surgery (ground floor) are housed. The two shorter sides of the rectangular building, including the one that faces the road, are of featureless concrete made on site and lack windows. The longer, north-facing elevation is constructed of panels of hollow, clear polycarbonate filled with granulated Styrofoam; these cannot be seen through but allow light to penetrate. Only the south-facing wall, which overlooks the courtyard space, is glazed. On this side privacy is provided by an outer, three-storey screen consisting of a steel frame that supports closely spaced, high-tension, stainless-steel wires up which fast-growing ivies climb. Like Ivy Structure, this house illustrates the parity that Ban seeks between outside and inside spaces.

The concept of a domestic architectural style that allows for a greater continuity between exterior and interior spaces was originally developed in the first half of the twentieth century by the German architect Mies van der Rohe. In his design completed in 1951 for the Farnsworth House in Illinois, he replaced solid masonry walls with glass curtain walls. This house also illustrates van der Rohe's idea of "universal space." A fluid interior space is achieved by the use of a continuous, uninterrupted roof, and dividing walls are replaced by free-standing partitions and furniture. Shigeru Ban has extended van der Rohe's idea in his Ivy House to develop his concept

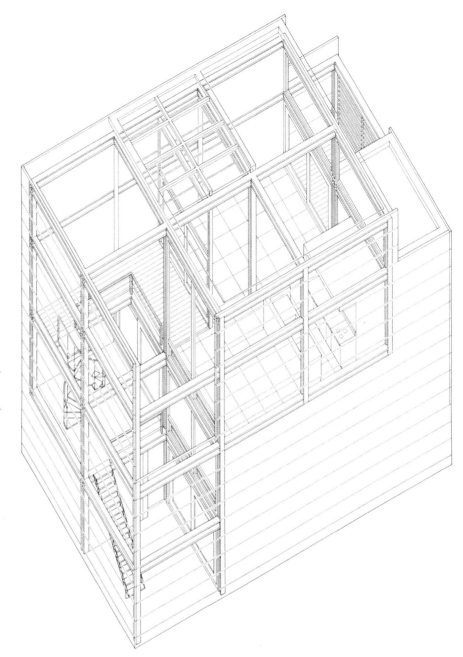

HOUSE, HIGASHI-OSAKA, TOKYO, JAPAN

ARCHITECT: **WARO KISHI**

◄ A view from the bottom of the rear courtyard shows a steel staircase leading to a spiral one that links the middle and upper levels. Glass walls and a glass roof fill the space with light.

▲ This isometric drawing shows the rear of the building, and the four-storey courtyard space can be seen in the bottom-left corner. On the upper levels the space expands to the full width of the rear of the building and includes decked terraces on to which rooms open.

COURTYARD HOUSING,
MATOSINHOS, PORTUGAL
ARCHITECT: EDUARDO
SOUTA DE MOURA

▼ Each garden is a variation
of a simple composition
that comprises swimming
pool, deck, lawn, path,
and planting. In each
case the planting is
restricted to a narrow
border that lines the walls.

► Cross-sectional drawings
of a sample apartment
and its garden suggest
that the architect assigned
equal importance to the
two complementary spaces.

of the "universal floor," in which both interior and exterior spaces are continuous.

Waro Kishi is another Japanese architect who is interested in setting up a dialogue between inner and outer voids set within an architectural whole. Both Ban and Kishi are well aware of the need to maximize space in the overcrowded towns and cities of Japan. Kishi's design for a house in Higashi-Osaka had to make the most of a narrow in-fill site situated among railway lines and overhead cables in a congested neighbourhood typical of Tokyo. The house, built in 1997, is of an introverted design, looking in on itself rather than opening on to its urban surroundings. The living areas are separated from the outside world by a combination of fixed and sliding, opaque and translucent, screens and roof panels. Exterior grilles

and mesh panels allow natural light to filter through to the interior of the house.

The building is basically a four-storey steel frame painted white. The steel skeleton is three bays deep and two bays wide, with an additional shallow bay at the front as a barrier between the home and the street. Most of the rear portion of the house is left as a void. Open to the sky, it allows light and air into the living spaces that connect with it. This outside room, which is essentially a courtyard, contains a solitary, wide-spreading tree and an open steel staircase that gives access from the compact ground-floor rooms to the more spacious and airier upper living quarters.

The staircase leads to a spiral staircase that links the middle and upper levels of the house, and here the steel-frame building becomes more transparent.

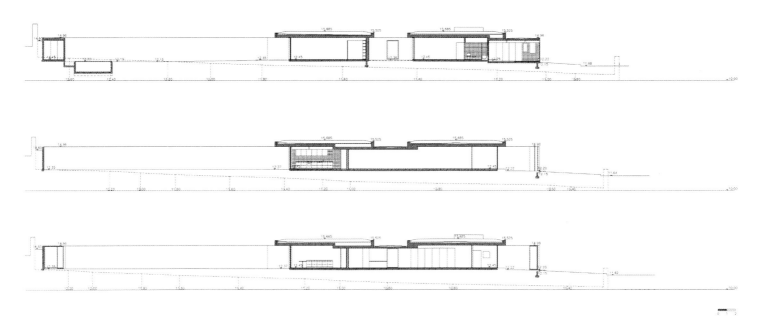

Glass walls replace the more solid partitions of the ground-floor rooms, and the house is capped with an open and translucent roof. On the upper floors, small, decked, open-air courts form private external living areas. In short the house opens inwards and upwards. Owing to the limited size of the site, the four-storey external space had to be functional rather than solely an outdoor leisure space, and there was no room for a pleasure garden in the traditional sense. The single tree is the only living element, its structure providing a visual foil to the architecture's geometry, and its leafy canopy modulating the natural light that enters from above.

An overcrowded urban environment was not a problem for the Portuguese architect Eduardo Souta de Moura when he was commissioned to design a residential development at Matosinhos, near Porto, Portugal. The site was the former vegetable garden of a grand villa, and the architect was able to provide the new properties with large, walled gardens and courtyards. A distinctive feature of this development is Souta de Moura's desire to give outdoor and indoor living space equal status.

The Courtyard Housing project, as it is called, was completed in 1993 and comprises nine, single-storey dwellings. Their layout is almost identical, although the five larger and longer of the nine properties have a swimming pool each, whereas the others do not. All of the residences are bordered at the rear by the remainder of the villa's gardens, while the fronts look on to the adjacent harbour of Porto de Leixoes. The development could be described as ten walls defining nine plots, arranged in a staggered formation.

All of the dwellings have enclosed walled gardens and inner courtyards. Internally, low ceilings lead from front bedroom areas, past the inner courtyards,

THE HOUSE AT KORAMANGALA, TAMIL NADU, INDIA
ARCHITECT: **CHARLES CORREA**

▲ Bamboo blinds provide shade for the rooms that open on to the central courtyard garden. To prevent flooding of the house by rain in the wet season, the floor of the courtyard is lower than those of the adjoining rooms. At its centre the courtyard has a sunken pebbled area through which water drains away.

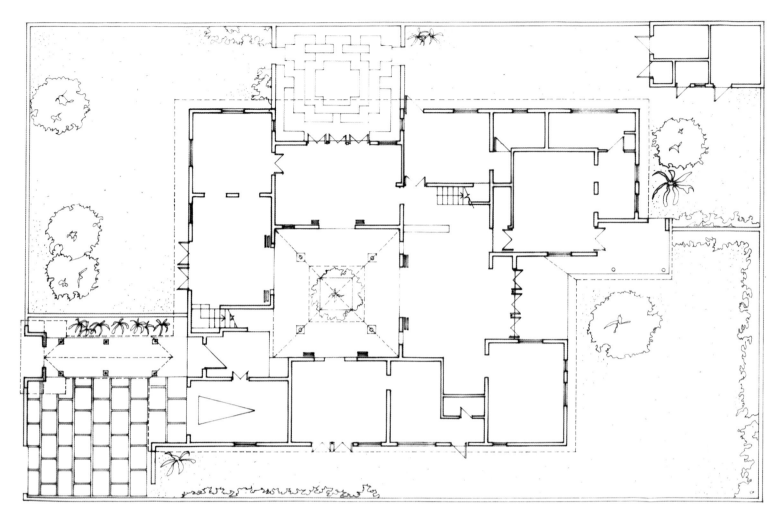

to rear living spaces that provide uninterrupted views of the garden. The white walls enclosing the garden, which are the same height as the buildings, continue through the interior of the dwellings, linking front to rear and separating them. This uninterrupted wall blurs the distinction between indoor and outdoor space, underlining the fact that both are equally important and have been conceived as part of an architectural whole. In some of the properties the walled garden space is larger than that of the interior living space, thereby giving the impression that the house is enclosed within the garden. Alternatively, the interior space can be read as simply a covered area between the garden walls, and the rear exterior space as can be seen just the largest room within these walls.

Souta de Moura's reduction of the architecture to horizontal and vertical planes shows the influence of the minimalist aesthetic. Charles Correa is influenced by a more ancient tradition. Born in India but trained as an architect in the USA, Correa returned to work in his native land, where the climate and local architecture have influenced the development of his own distinctive design style – most evident in the inclusion of outdoor rooms in his architecture. Responsive to the warm climate of India, he believes that the best place to be in the early mornings and late evenings is under an open sky.

India's climate makes outdoor living possible almost all year round. Historically, Indian architecture has always featured open-air spaces, in the form of verandas, terraces, and courtyards, with trees or pergolas often included to provide shade. Correa continues this tradition in his architecture, making outdoor rooms essential ingredients in his designs for both public and domestic buildings.

▲ This drawing shows the architect's ground plan for his house and studio. Informal in style, the house includes several outdoor "green" spaces within its walls. The central, Roman-style courtyard garden is the focus of the house, with four rooms opening on to it. The focal point of the garden itself is the single tree standing in a bed of pebbles in the middle.

Many of Correa's domestic houses are based on the traditional patio house common in India. The old Hindu houses of Tamil Nadu and Goa were often organized around small courtyards containing a single central tree or *tulsi* plant. The tree or plant provided shade in the courtyard, which in turn helped to ventilate the surrounding rooms. A central courtyard was to be an important element in Correa's own house and studio in Bangalore, known as the House at Koramangala and completed in 1973.

Here the courtyard is defined at each corner by a column, forming a simple portico or covered walkway. Rooms and corridors open on to the courtyard, at the centre of which is a pebble-filled depression containing a solitary *champa* tree. Bamboo screens fixed to the roof of the portico can be rolled down to provide shade and to separate it from the interior rooms. Instead of murals, as in the courtyards of the villas of Pompeii, framed paintings hang from the walls, and they seem to emphasize the idea that this roofless space is as much as a room as it is a garden. This is in keeping with Correa's belief that open-air spaces have spiritual benefits. For him, the sun is the origin of life, and we need to feel its presence.

The British architect Mark Guard has also included a courtyard as an integral part of his design for a house in Deptford, south London. He has developed the exterior space in a manner similar to that of Shigeru Ban by setting out to integrate interior and exterior spaces. In its use of plain surfaces of steel and sliding glass partitions, his architectural vocabulary is also similar to Ban's.

The house in Deptford, completed in 1995, stands on the site of a former car-repair workshop and is contained within the walls of the older building. The arrangement of the living accommodation reverses the norm by placing the bedrooms on the ground floor. In plan the house is divided into three parts, which are linked by a passageway that runs internally and externally from the front to the rear. In the first third of the property it opens on to the bedrooms and to stairs that leads up to the living rooms. In the second third it becomes external, passing under an open steel framework and flanked on both sides by free-standing walls. The spaces between the walls provide glimpses of planted courtyards on either side. One part of the path is bordered by a long pond with stepping-stone access to the main courtyard garden. The principal bedroom looks on to this, and a floor-to-ceiling window, which can be fully opened, allows complete integration of house and garden.

In keeping with the style of the house, the courtyard garden is minimal in content, A gravel surface reflects the plain concrete finish of the interior floors, and planting is restricted to a group of birches, *Betula jacquemontii*, with their distinctive white bark and delicate foliage through which light filters.

In the final third of the site, on the far side of the main courtyard, is a separate studio, which, like the main bedroom, can also be fully opened on to the courtyard. Steps to the rear of the studio lead to a rooftop terrace above. In effect two-thirds of the architectural space of the house is given over to exterior spaces or enclosed garden rooms. The building's external walls give protection and privacy, but within them the inner and outer spaces are able to merge as a continuous architectural space.

The Japanese architect Tadao Ando's Kidosaki House in Setagaya-Ku, Tokyo, also achieves an equality between exterior and interior spaces, but his method is very different from that of Guard. Born in Japan in 1941, Ando is self-educated and learned about architecture by studying the traditional buildings of Japan, particularly those in Kyoto, where he visited temples, shrines, and tea houses. In the 1960s, with money earned from a successful boxing career, he travelled in Europe and the USA and on his return formed Tadao Ando Architect and Associates in Osaka. By the 1990s he had won all of the four main prizes for architectural achievement – the only living architect to achieve this feat – including the Pritzer Prize, the architectural equivalent of the Nobel Prize. Ando's buildings are known for the power of their restrained design, a style that combines simple, geometric forms with plain, functional surfaces. His almost puritanical approach to the design of buildings reflects a respect for the discipline of traditional Japanese architecture.

Built in 1986, the Kidosaki House consists of a central cube-shaped dwelling confined within a two-

▶ At night, with the master bedroom illuminated, the floor-to-ceiling window is almost invisible, making the interior accommodation and the courtyard garden seem to be one continuous space. To the right, flanked by a shallow water channel, is the inside-outside path that connects the front of the house to the studio at the rear.

LEONARD HOTEL, LONDON, UK

LANDSCAPE ARCHITECT:
PAUL COOPER

◄ Choosing the right lighting for this garden room was important. Sophisticated but subtle, it is intended, like the paintings on the walls and the existing window, to prolong the illusion that the planted space is just another indoor room – until the lack of a roof gives the game away.

storey outer wall that defines the boundary of the slightly off-square site. In the irregularly shaped space between the outer wall and the central cube are additional living units. In this house within a house there are three apartments, all on different levels and each with an adjoining external space in the form of a courtyard or a planted roof garden. In plan the house is a series of rectangular walled spaces, an essay in solids and voids in which the spaces open to the sky are courtyard gardens and those covered are the living accommodation.

The ground-floor space on the northern side is a courtyard entrance, and in the southern corner is an L-shaped garden courtyard planted with birch trees. (In order to maintain a link with the original site, Ando planted the same variety of tree that formerly grew there.) His concrete-walled outdoor rooms are conceived as places within the architecture of the building where exposure to the weather is regarded as an intrinsic traditional feature and an essential promoter of social interaction.

When an additional communal area was needed for a hotel in central London, a decision was made to make one that was likewise "exposed to the elements" with the roof as the chosen location. When owners of the Leonard Hotel asked me to design a roof garden, I was surprised to discover that the site was simply a top-floor room with the roof left off. A sash window in one corner added to the incongruity of the place, and this confusion between room and roof garden is what I attempted to reinforce in my design. The open-air room was conceived during a renovation of the hotel that included the addition of an extra floor. Patio-style doors open on to the space, which, despite its small size – 5m (16½ft) by 3m (10ft) – was envisaged by the proprietors as an outdoor sitting area for guests and a place in which to hold social functions. As the garden room had to accommodate as many people as possible, fitted seating was essential, and the need to keep a clear central area meant that planting had to be confined to the perimeters.

I decided that the style and look of the space should relate to the Edwardian-style interior decor of the hotel, with walls adorned with paintings from

that period. In the garden room the hotel's luxurious interior is echoed by a floor of polished limestone and Classical-style, stainless-steel columns that support climbing plants. As in the guest rooms, the garden room is decorated with paintings, but in a contemporary style based on plant forms. Mesh panels fixed to the walls are designed to encourage the planting to become living wallpaper and so transform the space into a "green room."

A "green room" of a very different character and aim was created by Bernard Saint-Denis and Peter Fianu at the Festival International des Jardins, in Quebec's Jardins de Métis, during the summer of 2000. "The Living Room" was designed to highlight contradictions in our contemporary relationship with nature. For example, as our environment is threatened by industrial and economic growth we have become more ecologically aware, and as our lifestyle has become increasingly technological there has been an upturn in the art of gardening. These opposing trends are expressed in the garden through a witty mutation of the norm in which walls become grassy mounds

KIDOSAKI HOUSE,
SETAGAYA-KU, TOKYO,
JAPAN

ARCHITECT: **TADAO ANDO**

◀ This space is what the
Japanese describe as
an entrance garden
courtyard, with its
staircases leading to the
adjoining apartments.
The natural light passing
through the canopies of
the trees dapples the plain
concrete walls and slate
floor with patterns of light
and shade. A single
container provides the
only sculptural interest
in this minimalist design.

and a wooden floor is suggested by a "lawn" of wood chips. This compact and private green space has no windows; once inside, one is shut off from reality. With a touch of irony, a television set projecting from one of the grassy walls provides visitors with their only view of the world beyond.

Less radical but just as inventive is the use of exterior enclosures in the design of a house in Arizona. Here, more conventional walls are used to protect gardens and outdoor living spaces from the harsh climate of the surrounding Sonoran Desert.

The house, built in 1998, was created by its owners, the Stitelers, with the help of a local architect. The Stitelers had been inspired by the work of the late Mexican architect Luis Barragán, whose style is identifiable by its almost monastic simplicity and its use of plain walls painted in vivid colours.

Born in 1902, Barragán trained as an engineer; although he later became an architect and the spiritual leader of Mexican minimalist architecture, he regarded himself first and foremost as a landscape architect. Even in his early designs for houses, which reflected Spanish and Moroccan influences as well as the more contemporary style of the French architect Le Corbusier, he was concerned with the relationship of the house to the landscape. By the 1940s he had designed several gardens where he experimented with the juxtaposition of stone walls and horizontal planes with water in pools, channels and man-made waterfalls. Later, influenced by the brightly coloured houses of his native Guadalajara, he introduced painted, rendered walls into his designs. Many of his commissions were for ranches, where he would use bright colours, trees, and water to create a sense of theatre. The architectural elements of his gardens are more important than any profusion of planting, which is often reduced to a single species of tree. By borrowing from the formal language of Barragán, the Stitelers were adopting an architectural style that would allow their house to extend outwards and to embrace external spaces.

Less confident in horticultural matters, the owners of the Arizona house appointed the landscape architect Steve Martino, who has earned a reputation for creating gardens suitable for, and in sympathy with, desert environments. Like Barragán, Martino began as an architect but switched to landscape architecture in the mid-1970s; since then he has often

worked with architects to advise on the placing of new houses in the context of the desert environment. He is also known for his use of brightly coloured walls as backdrops to his restrained planting schemes.

The garden itself is contained within a series of compartments, some of which are quite small and completely enclosed, while others are larger and more open. One space includes an outdoor fireplace and is intended as an outdoor dining area. In another, a water trough reflects the sky. Window-like apertures in the colourful sheltering walls frame views and link the secluded inner garden spaces to the desert landscape beyond. Other spaces contain the owners'

rose collection and raised vegetable beds. The result is a series of roofless "rooms" that form an intermediate zone between the house and the desert.

Martino is highly respected for his knowledge of desert plants and their use, and frequently chooses plants for functional reasons, to create enclosure and refuge, or to cast cooling shade. The Stitelers' design brief was to reclaim the desert and bring it into the garden. Summer temperatures in the Arizona desert soar above 38°C (100.4°F), and annual rainfall rarely exceeds 18cm (7in), so Martino selected plants native to the desert because these tolerate the extreme climate and poor soil.

◀ The designers' concept drawing for "The Living Room" reveals that the garden's proposed location is a woodland grove. The surrounding natural vegetation is adopted and exploited to reinforce the feeling of enclosure and the incongruity of what lies within the four grass walls of the "room."

HOUSE, SONORAN DESERT, ARIZONA, USA
LANDSCAPE ARCHITECT: **STEVE MARTINO**

◄ The brightly coloured walls that enclose this unroofed courtyard keep the wilderness at bay, although the desert is visible through a window-like aperture. A simple water trough adds to the charm of the outdoor room, which even has an outdoor fireplace.

THE HAWKINSON GARDEN, PHOENIX, USA
LANDSCAPE ARCHITECT: **STEVE MARTINO**

► In the lower garden brightly coloured, rendered walls define garden rooms and provide seclusion from the city streets. A water feature creates refreshing sounds and acts as a secret entrance to two further rooms concealed between the pink and red walls.

For a house in a more urban desert environment Martino used walls and screens for a different purpose. In his design for the Hawkinson Garden, in Phoenix, Arizona, colourful walls create a secluded garden for a house that is situated in a heavily populated part of the city. A fountain blocks out the city's noise, and curved walls focus the sound of the water in the main sitting area. Further enclosures are contained within the garden. A water channel leading from the fountain is a secret entrance to two outdoor rooms – one a shower room, the other a storage area.

Similar in spirit, and located on the outskirts of "the city in the desert," as Phoenix is sometimes known, is the Schall House. Designed by the American architect Wendell Burnette and completed in 1999, the building looks like the hull of a ship when viewed from the road. However, despite its unconventional appearance, it is in fact based on the traditional Spanish or Spanish-American patio dwelling. This type of house is a predominantly urban form built around a paved courtyard that can be used for a variety of outdoor activities.

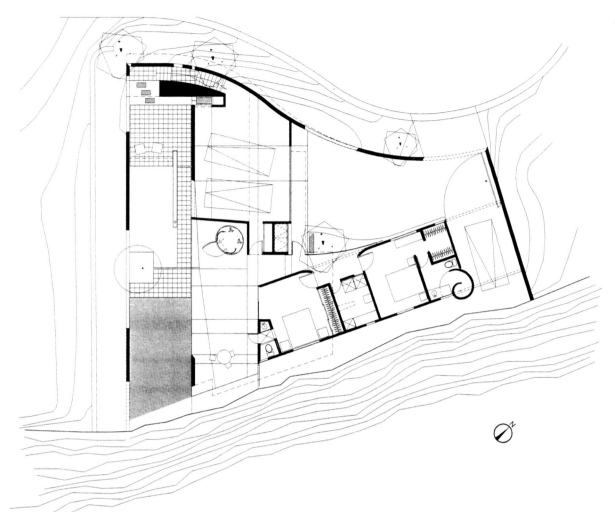

◄ The plan of the ground floor reveals that the shape of the Schall House is determined by the line of the nearby road and by the natural contours of the site. The inner courtyard is on the left, and the shaded area is the swimming pool. The pool is enclosed on the south-west boundary but remains open along the more secluded south-east side. In the north-west corner (top right), is the entrance courtyard.

THE SCHALL HOUSE, PHOENIX, USA

ARCHITECT: **WENDELL BURNETTE**

◄ The partly covered terrace with its high-tech lift overlooks the swimming pool and the planted patio. The stark, white, untextured walls of the building and patio contrast with the rugged terrain of the surrounding desert, which is visible through openings designed to frame the view.

Situated on a sloping site at the end of a cul-de-sac, the house stands at the point where the suburban landscape gives way to desert. As well as being influenced by the patio dwelling, the architect drew inspiration from the domestic architecture of North Africa, a region that has a dry and harsh climate similar to that of Arizona. The combination of these influences has produced a house that hides within its walls a secret realm, peaceful and protected, with a cooling swimming pool and lush planting. While the enclosed courtyard gives concealment and shelter, three large openings in the walls give dramatic views of the surrounding desert.

A gravelled entrance courtyard with a water feature leads to the elevated inner patio. Like its historical precedents, this enclosed space is the centre of the house, and has a similar function to the traditional patio; however, its design belongs very much to today. This fact is highlighted by the sleek, ovoid lift, which travels between the patio and the overhanging floor above. White walls, rectangular forms, and precise lines define this unquestionably modernist space, which has been described as "a fusion of light, water and greenery."

The Mexican architect Ricardo Legorreta also incorporates outdoor spaces, such as courtyards and terraces, into his domestic architecture. His decision to do so was in part a result of his being advised by his fellow countryman Luis Barragán that he ought to pay more attention to the landscaping because it is an "integral part of architecture." Legorreta has also been influenced by Mexico's vernacular architecture, in particular the simple forms of pre-Columbian architecture and the colourful walls of traditional

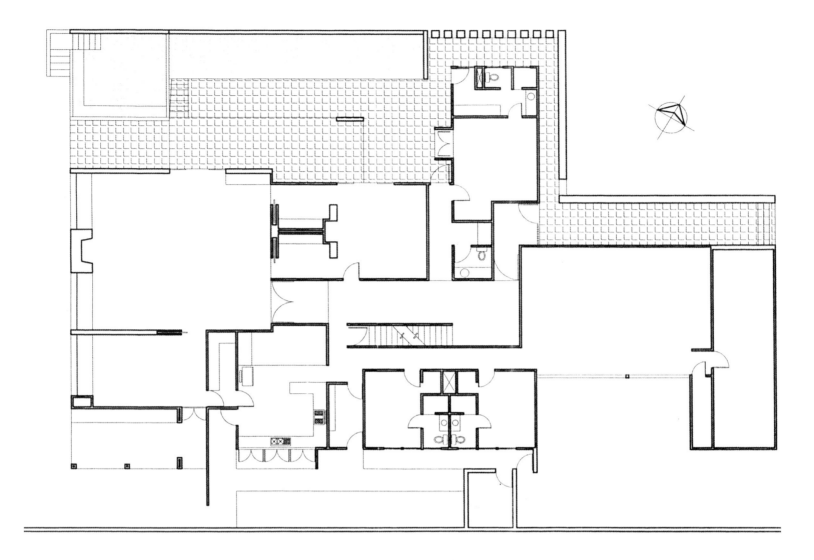

THE MONTALBAN HOUSE, HOLLYWOOD HILLS, USA

ARCHITECT: **RICARDO LEGORRETA**

▲ This floor plan shows the open-air courtyard terrace on the north-west side of the house and the open terrace on the opposite side of the building. The inclusion of these two generously proportioned spaces underlines the importance customarily assigned to outdoor living areas in the domestic architecture of hot and dry climates.

▶ In the foreground is the partly covered outdoor living room, containing bespoke furniture, while beyond are two lap pools and fountains. The brightly coloured walls give architectural definition to the external spaces and include openings to provide users of the elevated terrace with views of the landscape beyond.

village dwellings. In Mexican architecture the wall has always been important, not just structurally, aesthetically, or as the means by which the limit of a property is defined, but as a symbol of protection.

In 1985 Legorreta was commissioned by the Mexican film actor Ricardo Montalban to build a house in the Hollywood Hills, California. The client wanted the design to reflect Mexican architectural heritage in a contemporary manner. The site was a sloping hilltop, and Legoretta borrowed the high, solid walls of ranch-style Mexican architecture to establish the stepped house firmly on the hill and to conceal a private outdoor space. This terrace, exterior but incorporated into the building behind colourful walls, includes an open-sided, fully furnished living room, a fountain, and a pool.

**HOUSE K, MELBOURNE,
AUSTRALIA**

ARCHITECTS: **BOCHSLER
AND PARTNERS**

▶ An internal ornamental
pool forms part of a
continuous water feature
that separates the public
and private spaces of this
house. A stepping-stone
path, seen in the
foreground, provides
the means of crossing the
pool. A water garden is
an unusual choice for
an interiorscape in a
private dwelling.

The enclosed garden rooms created by Wendell Burnette and Ricardo Legorreta are essentially updates of the traditional courtyard versions. The Australian architects Bochsler and Partners have brought the garden into the house in a more subtle and ambiguous way. In a property known simply as House K, at Caulfield, Melbourne, the architects have included an ornamental water garden that links both exterior and interior spaces. The water, in the form of a shallow canal, bisects the house. Starting externally, it then passes under a full-length window to enter the house, where it is bridged by a carpeted walkway, before returning outside. Within the property, the pool, planted with water lilies and other aquatics, serves as a decorative division between the living rooms and the ground-floor bedroom area. Floor-to-ceiling windows and reflections in the glass and the water conspire to create a spatial illusion in which it is sometimes difficult to see where the inside ends and the outside begins.

Bochsler and Partners have created several domestic properties featuring water gardens. All of their domestic commissions are identified by a single letter, and L and G, two more houses in Melbourne, also feature water both externally and internally. In House L, a lily pond penetrates the house, with a wall of glass being the only barrier, and in G an outdoor swimming pool links visually with an internal lap pool. In both designs, water and house are inseparable, helped by modern construction methods and strong panes of glass, which, when immersed in the pools, act as air-tight seals between the outside and inside. In the hot summers of south-east Australia the water gardens, inside and outside, bring coolness and tranquillity to these houses. In performing this function they are a modern equivalent of the water gardens that were essential elements of the courtyards of Moorish Spain, such as the gardens of the Alhambra in Granada.

The concept of the enclosed garden room has been adopted by many architects and landscape designers as a means of integrating gardens within buildings. Some, like Bochsler and Partners, have broken away from the courtyard tradition, while others, including the architect Tadao Ando and the

PETTIT HOUSE, SYDNEY, AUSTRALIA
ARCHITECTS: **ANCHER MORTLOCK WOOLLEY**

▶ In this single-storey contemporary dwelling two internal courtyards connect with the rooms and corridors. Neither courtyard is bigger than a small room, and each one contains an ornamental pond. The two pools are different in shape and style, but both are surrounded by mixed grasses and cycads that contrast with the straight lines of the architecture and bring the natural world inside.

landscape designer Toru Mitani have sought to reinvent it. In some cases this has been because the enclosed spaces are defined not by the walls of a house but by a corporate building's architecture. This is true of Mitani's courtyard garden for the Setonaikai Broadcasting Station at Takamatsu, Japan.

As a result of development of the media building, a neglected, overgrown corner of the site had become enclosed within a new wing and was overlooked by an entrance lobby and cafeteria. A formerly external landscape had become a courtyard garden by default,

and Mitani responded to this by retaining some of the existing cherry trees and evergreen shrubs and adding no more than a new floor surface. He paved the area with granite slabs, leaving holes to accommodate the roots of the trees. Additional interest at ground level is provided by a row of small pots used in summer to burn incense as a way of discouraging insects. When the trees are in leaf, their canopies provide shade and create ever-changing shadow patterns on the granite floor. Mitani has transformed a disused space into a modern courtyard by the simplest of means.

SETONAIKAI BROADCASTING STATION, TAKAMATSU, JAPAN

LANDSCAPE ARCHITECT:
TORU MITANI AND STUDIO ON SITE

▲ Squares of striped two-tone granite paving laid out in a grid reinvigorated a neglected urban space. The lines between the squares are filled with granite chippings.

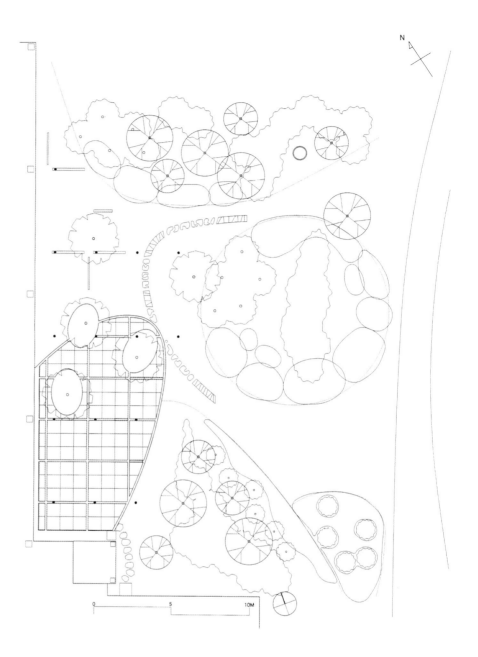

▲ The plan of the broadcasting station shows the designer's proposal to incorporate many of the existing plants and trees, with some new additions, in a simple, organic design. In this way the character of theoriginal neglected site was retained, and the only new hard landscaping was a terrace and a stepping-stone path. The paved terrace is defined by a curvilinear line that links it sympathetically to the surrounding soft landscaping, while the square grid pattern of the granite paving makes a connection with the angular, architectural lines of the adjacent building.

The history of gardens under glass begins with the greenhouse. Used today mainly as a place in which to grow and propagate plants, it was first developed in Britain in the sixteenth century to overwinter tender greens, and this gave it its name. In the seventeenth century Louis XIV believed that he could use them in the gardens of his palace at Versailles to defy the restrictions imposed by the seasons. Tender orange plants were planted directly into the ground, and, with the approach of winter, temporary greenhouses were built over them.

During the eighteenth century an increasing interest in gardening led ambitious gardeners to look to warmer countries for more exotic greenery. This was particularly true in Britain, where tender plants such as bays, oranges, and myrtles were imported and had to be protected during the winter. This influx of plants from abroad, brought in by both amateur gardeners and plant-collecting botanists, called for the development of the greenhouse. Until the end of the eighteenth century glasshouses were heated by hot air drawn in through flues. In the nineteenth century this system was replaced by a much more easily managed one that used circulating hot water. By the middle of the century new building methods enabled far more ambitious greenhouses to be created, with iron frames replacing wooden ones. The iron-and-glass Palm House at the Royal Botanic

LONGWOOD GARDENS, PENNSYLVANIA, USA

LANDSCAPE ARCHITECT: **ISABELLE GREENE**

▲ Greene's dry garden in the Conservatory at Longwood is intended to demonstrate which types of plant will tolerate drought conditions and includes cacti, succulents, and palms. The design is not just informative – it is an elegant planting scheme that explores colour, texture, and form.

▶ The Conservatory's ornamental garden acts as a winter garden and, with its fountains and informal sitting areas, it is an attractive and popular social facility. A "chandelier" of hanging baskets provides a splash of colour amid the canopies of the trees.

Gardens in Kew, London, was some 110m (361ft) in length and tall enough to accommodate palm trees of forest size. Warm–water heating kept temperatures at a constant 27°C (81°F), and moisture was provided by a sprinkler system. Kew became a respected scientific and horticultural institution, symbolized by its two great greenhouses: the Palm House and the later Temperate House, created by Decimus Burton and Richard Turner respectively.

Botanical gardens continue to invest in glasshouses, and the leading architects of the day are often employed to design them. In recently built public glasshouses the science-based tendency to present simply a catalogue of plants has been replaced by a desire to create a comprehensible and cohesive interior landscape. Some of these schemes have been designed by internationally renowned landscape architects.

The Conservatory at Longwood Gardens, Pennsylvania, houses interior landscapes created by Isabelle Greene, including a dry garden with plants associated with the desert regions of North America. Greene's design work is characterized by its seemingly effortless planting style and use of natural forms. This is particularly evident in the dry garden, in which sculptural cacti, palms, and succulents emerge from a patterned carpet of ground cover.

**THE GREAT GLASSHOUSE,
NATIONAL BOTANIC
GARDEN OF WALES,
GWENT, UK**
ARCHITECTS: **FOSTER AND
PARTNERS**
LANDSCAPE DESIGNER:
KATHRYN GUSTAFSON

◄ The vast arches of the Great Glasshouse soar over an arid landscape where sparse vegetation is the result of a simulation of the hot and dry conditions of Mediterranean-type ecosystems. Plant species will be added over a long period of time to imitate the natural cycle of growth and renewal.

The Great Glasshouse at the National Botanic Garden of Wales belongs firmly to the twenty-first century, and involved in its creation were a leading architect and a leading landscape designer. The building, designed by the British architectural firm of Foster and Partners, is set into a natural hill, and its gently domed, oval shape nestles comfortably and unobtrusively within the soft contours of the Gwent countryside. Visible in glimpses from afar, the high-tech steel-and-glass structure is an eye-catching addition to the landscape of this part of South Wales.

In technical terms the shape is an elliptical torus, 95m (312ft) long by 55m (180ft) wide, and tilted seven degrees on its axis to obtain maximum sunlight. The roof contains 785 panes of glass and covers an area of 4500 sq m (48,440 sq ft). When it was completed in 2000 it was the world's largest single-span glasshouse. The technology inside is designed to provide an environment suitable for plants associated with a Mediterranean-type climate. Characterized by cool, moist winters and hot, dry summers, such climatic conditions occur in many other parts of the world. To simulate the windy conditions associated with such regions, the glasshouse has powerful, high-mounted fans.

The impressive architecture and operating systems were given an interior landscape to match, in the person of Kathryn Gustafson. The importance of employing an inventive and experienced landscape

EDEN PROJECT, NEAR ST AUSTELL, CORNWALL, UK
CONCEPT: **TIM SMIT**

ARCHITECTS: **NICHOLAS GRIMSHAW AND PARTNERS**

LANDSCAPE DESIGNERS: **LAND USE CONSULTANTS**

▶ Huge geodesic bubbles enclose a subtropical forest in the English countryside. The bold architecture reflects the engineering required to sustain this luxuriant artificial environment.

designer is visible in the design. Although she had to identify several different geographical areas within this work, Gustafson has created a single coherent landscape in which the roof of the glasshouse becomes the sky. The multi-level landscape is a sandstone terrain and features an informal gravel path that descends a central ravine. The path is bordered by a series of stepped, rocky terraces and gravel scree slopes. These slopes provide a wide range of habitats, with a variety of light and shade and varying moisture levels to suit the different types of plants. The ravine drops to a depth of 5.5m (18ft), where it culminates in a waterfall angled so that it is in shadow in the morning and in full sun by early afternoon.

The landscape contains six different geographical areas, including the Cape region of South Africa and the chaparral of southern California, as well as the Mediterranean region itself, but as the visitor moves from one "country" to another, the feeling is one of walking through an integrated environment. Planting is also coherent, arranged to create a sense of density, form, and colour at the same time as presenting a wide range of species in their correct context. This glasshouse is successful because it combines a deceptively simple architecture with a thoughtful interior landscape, which, in addition to being informative, can also be appreciated as an original landscape in its own right.

The Eden Project, in Cornwall, conceived by the entrepreneur Tim Smit and opened in 2001, offers a different kind of experience. It aims to encourage a greater understanding of the natural world and inspire a desire to look after it. The plant displays have political agendas and are used to tell stories about the food we eat, the clothes we wear, and the weather we either enjoy or suffer. The overarching intention is to

MELBOURNE MUSEUM, MELBOURNE, AUSTRALIA

ARCHITECTS: DENTON CORKER MARSHALL

◀ Looking into the Gallery of Life from one of the internal streets of the new museum is like peering into a waterless aquarium. Containing real flora and fauna, the gallery presents an idealized version of the natural world that is perhaps more palatable than the reality. At the same time, in the context of a museum, nature is presented as something to be preserved and protected like a work of art or an historic relic.

▲ The glasshouse of the Gallery of Life projects forward beyond the main body of the museum, towards the sun and the surrounding park. This museum marks a development in museum design. Here a glasshouse displaying living natural history is combined with galleries containing fossils and ancient artifacts.

show that environmental awareness is about the quality of life at all levels. According to its manifesto, the Eden Project is not a botanical garden but a theatre in which our relationship with the plant world is played out.

The Eden Project is contained within a series of interlinked geodesic domes situated in a disused china-clay quarry. The design seems to have been inspired by science fiction, but this is far from the truth, which has more to do with practical necessity and the demands of the unusual site. The vast greenhouses had to be located in a sunny spot at the base of the north wall of the quarry. The architects, Nicholas Grimshaw and Partners, first considered a lean-to structure, but the quarry wall was too uneven. This type of structure would also have needed heavy components, which would have been difficult to lower into the quarry. A lighter and more economic alternative was a single large geodesic dome, but such a structure would have been difficult to integrate with the contours of the quarry and would not easily have divided up into the different climatic zones required. The solution was a line of smaller, intersecting geodesic domes, made out of two-dimensional hexagons and pentagons, which were squeezed into

one another and pushed into the irregularly shaped site between the cliff at the top of the quarry and the base. The geodesic grid was scaled according to the size of each dome, making each as light as possible. These are the world's largest lean-to geodesic domes, yet they weigh only slightly more than the air they contain.

The hexagons that form the largest of the domes are 11m (36ft) wide and could not be spanned by a single pane of glass. Glass would also have been too heavy for the structure, especially as it would have to have been double-glazed. Instead the "windows" are made from a transparent material called ethyltetrafluorethylene. This light, flexible film is bonded to form transparent cushions that are kept inflated by a constant supply of air. The flexible pipes that supply the cushion roof panels – as well as the ducts of the heating and ventilation system – are all clearly visible and add to the drama of the space.

Inside the enormous bubbles of an area called the Humid Tropics Biome, the rainforest planting will be able to grow to its full height, although the biome is not a complete ecosystem since there are no captive animals within it. Despite the advantage of an inherited multi-level site, the interior landscaping is not as well conceived as that of the National Botanical Garden of Wales. Paths weave up through the planting to a waterfall at the top, but the attempt to recreate a naturalistic landscape is unconvincing and this, coupled with the project's desire to tell stories and communicate its "message," makes for a disjointed experience. Although the architecture's delicate spherical mesh high above is forgotten when

RAINFOREST SHOWROOM
HIALEAH, FLORIDA, USA
ARCHITECTS: **SITE**

◄ Water streams down the glass wall of a greenhouse built across the full width of the front of a BEST Products store. This wall of water helps to maintain the moist climate needed by the indigenous subtropical trees and plants inside.

one is inside; the architectural achievement of Grimshaw and his team should not be overlooked.

The Melbourne Museum, in Melbourne, Australia, designed by the Denton Corker Marshall partnership and completed in 1999, was an architecturally impressive glasshouse that contains not only living plants but also birds. The museum is located on a site adjacent to the nineteenth-century Royal Exhibition Building, which, when erected in 1880, was one of the largest architectural structures in Australia. The museum was begun in 1994, and the architects who won the competition to design it decided to reflect in a contemporary fashion the dynamism of the older iron-and-glass building.

On the north side of the museum are the main exhibition areas, at the centre of which is the large glasshouse of the Gallery of Life. The cantilevered roof of the glasshouse dominates the rest of the building as it soars upwards and outwards to project over the park at the entrance to the museum. The Gallery of Life, with its collection of indigenous Australian wildlife, is viewed from within the museum, where twin-level internal streets run alongside the glass walls.

▲ A sketch drawing of the front elevation of the BEST store shows the subtropical garden paradise envisaged in detail by the designer. In reality this was created by the plants that were already growing on the site. The double doors open on to a glazed passageway through which customers walk to reach the store behind.

RIO SHOPPING CENTER,
ATLANTA, USA
ARCHITECTS:**BERNARDO
FORT BRESCIA OF
ARQUITECTONICA**
LANDSCAPE DESIGNER:
MARTHA SCHWARTZ

◄ Gilt frogs guard the
rectangular black pool that
adjoins the covered square
plaza at the rear of the
shopping mall. With its
unorthodox sculptural
elements, this landscape
is an unashamedly modern
design for a modern
commercial environment.

Nature conservation was the unlikely inspiration for the design of a new merchandising showroom for North America's BEST Products (*pages 77–80*). Designed by SITE, an environmentally aware and radical architectural group based in New York City, it was one of a number of showrooms created by the practice for BEST. SITE's innovative showrooms for BEST were sponsored by the company's owners, Sydney and Frances Lewis, who, as keen collectors of contemporary art, were eager to bring art into the public domain. Instead of simply placing art objects in front of their shop buildings, they employed SITE to transform the fronts and entrances of their new

showrooms into works of art. In each case SITE took a characteristically box-shaped building and used it as a vehicle for the firm's anarchic architectural ideas, which often included a narrative element.

The BEST Rainforest Showroom in Hialeah, Florida, completed in 1979, is certainly more art than architecture but it also draws attention to environmental issues. The original site was covered with trees and rich vegetation, and SITE decided that the structure and content of the building's façade should speak of a conscientious desire to preserve the natural environment. The existing natural landscape, including palm trees, was carefully removed, stored,

► With its chequerboard
pattern and bright stripes,
the floor of the juice bar in the
plaza is a lively design, and
appropriate to an area that
is also used for dancing.
However, the planting,
in beds that continue the
colourful theme, is almost
overwhelmed by its
vibrant surroundings.

and preserved in a nursery during the construction of the Rainforest Showroom. When the building was complete, the former landscape was transferred to a large greenhouse that had been installed along the full length of the front wall of the store. A sealed glass passageway through the glasshouse provides the main access to the store. To simulate a moist subtropical environment, the glass front of the greenhouse was turned into a vast water wall. The water streaming down the panes of glass blurs the view of the garden and adds a sense of mystery. It also helps to keep the interior of the showroom cool.

In many large cities and towns throughout the world high-street shopping has been supplemented – or even replaced – by partially covered or fully enclosed retail environments. Referred to as "shopping centres" or "malls," they are designed to protect the shopper from the less pleasant extremes of the local climate or weather. Often air-conditioned and with glazed roofs, some of of these interior streets and plazas also have indoor gardens.

Sadly, very few shopping malls are blessed with landscape design of any quality or originality. The Rio Shopping Center in Atlanta, Georgia, designed by the Miami-based architect Bernardo Fort Brescia of Arquitectonica is an exception, not least because the landscaping was created by the maverick designer Martha Schwartz. Built in 1988, in mid-town Atlanta, the U-shaped shopping mall surrounds a central court. The rear third of this space, a two-storey area

HEIDELBERGER
DRUCKMASCHINEN,
HEIDELBERG, GERMANY
LANDSCAPE ARCHITECT:
GEORG PENKER

◀ This winter garden's square architectural space is countered by the central pool set on a diagonal line and the casually grouped trees. The central channel of water connects the internal winter garden with two identically sized external garden courts, one on either side of it.

used for eating and recreation, is roofed with a metal canopy. A diagonal bridge connects both wings of the mall at the upper level. Under the high canopy the floor of the plaza is set at a skew across a rectangular lake that covers two-thirds of the court. A sense of humour pervades the pool, which is filled with regimented lines of gilded frogs, sitting on the surface and appearing to look in worship towards a geodesic sphere of tubular-steel that acts as a signpost for the shopping centre.

The brief for the centre was to create a vibrant and exciting space that would encourage activity and attract passers-by. Schwartz has created a visually dynamic, pop-style environment by combining bold, primary colours with strong surface patterns. The covered plaza is dominated by colourful squares and circles. One circle contains plants, another a cocktail bar, and yet another defines a small grove of tall-growing bamboos. These circular forms echo the roof canopy, which is punctuated by two round holes. One hole allows the bamboo to grow to its full height; the other admits light and rain to sustain the planting in the other nearby circular bed.

Originally the "winter garden" was an outdoor area planted with conifers and shrubs, which provided winter interest through their foliage or flowers. In the nineteenth century the term became associated with the glasshouse or conservatory in which decorative, exotic, and less hardy plants were grown in a protected environment. Unlike the greenhouses found in botanical gardens, winter gardens were intended for pleasure rather than for the collection and preservation of rare and scientifically interesting specimens.

The introduction of the enclosed winter garden was made possible by the constructional advances seen in greenhouses such as those in Kew Gardens, London, and at Chatsworth House, Derbyshire. Impressive as these are, the pioneering building that lead to the modern concept of the winter garden was Joseph Paxton's Crystal Palace. Paxton had learned about glass architecture when designing the greenhouses at Chatsworth, but the Crystal Palace was a much more ambitious project. Prefabricated in iron and glass, it was erected to house the Great Exhibition of 1851.

PROVINCIAL INSURANCE BUILDING, DÜSSELDORF, GERMANY

LANDSCAPE ARCHITECT: **GEORG PENKER**

▲ The abundant planting in this corner of the winter garden contrasts with the restrained use of vegetation in the main plaza and thoroughfare. Bamboos create an exotic effect around the water feature, which irrigates the entire garden.

▶ The glazed roof makes the whole garden into a covered plaza or indoor street, complete with offices and a restaurant. In this all-weather environment staff and visitors can amble and relax. Trees are used to provide occasional shade and the striped paving helps to enliven the extensive floor area.

This "people's palace" in London's Hyde Park featured ornamental gardens with exotic plants from around the world, as well as decorative pools and spectacular fountains. The central cross-aisle was given a tall, glazed barrel vault in order to accommodate a number of large, mature elm trees. In its wake, sizeable and ornate iron-framed glasshouses and conservatories began to appear as additions to the houses of affluent Victorians, and the winter garden became an essential part of privileged nineteenth-century society.

The winter garden was also popular in nineteenth-century Germany and Austria. There was a famous example in Vienna in which the relatively warm and protected environment allowed less hardy plants, including camellias, to be grown, and as a result these varieties became very popular. Set out like an outdoor garden, it included walks, rockeries, and water features, as well as places to sit and relax. During the first half of the twentieth century winter gardens were exploited as venues for concerts and dancing; their garden aspect became marginalized, and eventually many of the original nineteenth-century examples were allowed to fall into decline.

Today the winter garden is making a comeback. The development during the twentieth century of the corporate headquarters and other office blocks based on modernist steel-and-glass architecture has reinvented the warm, bright glasshouse environment. These "corporate palaces" are the new winter gardens, with living plants incorporated to improve the working environment.

The Heidelberger Druckmaschinen company's Research and Development Centre in Heidelberg, Germany, features a large winter garden designed by the landscape architect Georg Penker and completed in 1990. Penker believes that buildings should be literally "green," and his views win enthusiastic support in Germany. The Research and Development Centre includes a series of internal and external garden spaces, and the landscape-design project involved the creation of roof gardens at fourth-floor level, as well as a first-floor winter garden that connects with external, courtyard-style rose and rhododendron gardens.

FEDERAL CHANCELLERY, BERLIN, GERMANY

ARCHITECTS: **CHARLOTTE FRANK AND AXEL SCHULTES OF FRANK SCHULTES WITT**

▲ In one of the series of winter gardens that punctuate the two wings of the five-storey building, the floor is below ground level which made it possible to construct a sloping and raised planting area bisected by a narrow flight of steps. Here the planting is restricted to ground cover and specimen trees, with foliage providing the only living colour.

▶ Each of the landscape designs is minimal in content. In this example, tinted gravel, isolated trees, and circular islands create a composition with a simplicity that echoes the Zen gardens of Japan.

**BECTON DICKINSON
IMMUNOCYTOMETRY
DIVISION BUILDING,
SAN JOSE, USA**
LANDSCAPE DESIGNER:
MARTHA SCHWARTZ

◀ Lattice-like partitions
made of wood and
planted with ficus vines
serve as "hedges" to break
up the long, featureless
atrium into "garden rooms."
The floor is composed of
coloured concrete in green
and black stripes, and
primary colours around
the pools enliven what
would otherwise be a dull,
unwelcoming passageway.

◀ The rectangular pools, each of which contains a circular planter, change in size as the "hedges" grow taller through the length of the atrium. Here, the hedges are low enough to sit on. Bright yellow ball fountains each shoot a single jet of water into the pool to provide visual and aural interest.

The interior winter garden is square in plan, and Penker has cleverly introduced diagonally orientated water channels and a central pool set into the granite paving to animate and add interest to the floor area. The formality of the space is also countered by the large and apparently randomly placed fig trees *Ficus benjamina*. The winter garden, which includes a cafeteria, provides the Research and Development Centre with a focus and a meeting place.

In another commercial project, which he completed for the Provincial Insurance Building in Düsseldorf in 1998, Penker developed the idea of the winter garden as an indoor plaza. The landscaped garden occupies an area under a high glass canopy that separates, and at the same time serves to connect, two office blocks facing each other. The design combines an open spacious "avenue" of trees and formal raised beds along the main thoroughfare which is linked to a more enclosed area of dense planting that evokes the jungle. Here, lush, subtropical planting, made possible by the greenhouse-like environment, surrounds a circular water feature. The main promenade is flanked along one side by an informal line of trees. Penker's enthusiasm for water, confined here to a narrow, curving "canal," is used as a means of animating and giving a sense of direction to the long, rectangular space.

The German Chancellery in Berlin, designed by Charlotte Frank and Axel Schultes of Frank Schultes Witt and completed in 2000, contains a series of winter gardens. The building has a central block containing the entrance lobby, a debating chamber, cabinet rooms, and the Chancellor's office. This block is flanked on two sides by wings that run parallel to each other, one containing parliamentary offices and the other a library. At regular intervals along the wings, the five-storey office and library accommodation is interrupted by a winter garden, where the gardens have glazed roofs and partially glazed outer walls. These gardens are climatically controlled by automatic louvres, which also reduce glare on sunny days. The office windows overlooking the gardens can be opened so that staff can enjoy the green spaces while working. Every garden is different in plan, but the planting in each one is drawn from a restricted palette of olive trees, grass, gravel, and ground-cover ivy.

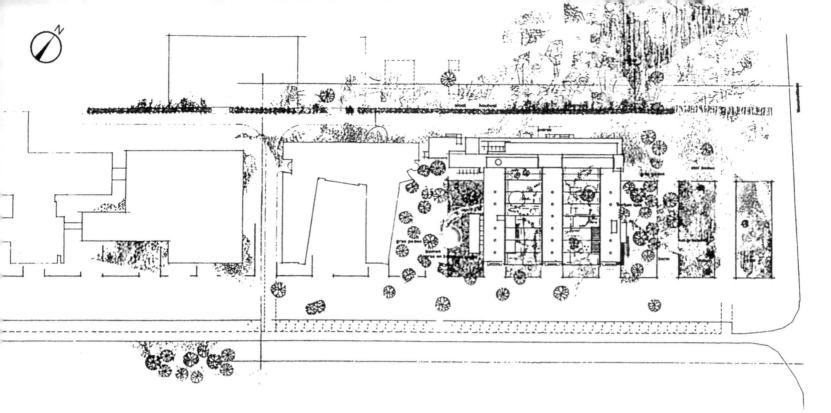

A path leading from an access door in the centre of the exterior, partially glazed, wall bisects all the gardens and echoes the ladder-like section of window that rises up above the door. In one garden the path is bordered by a sea of gravel punctuated by circular islands of ground cover and widely spaced trees; in another the floor is sunken, with the central path becoming stepped as it drops down between two sloping, rectangular planted areas, each containing a single tree and dense ground-cover ivy.

Any glass-roofed architectural space acts like a greenhouse and can be a place where plants will thrive if they are adequately watered and tended. If space is limited, but an instant effect is required, the choice of plants and how they are used must be carefully considered. Large specimen plants, although useful when immediate results are desired, could easily outgrow a small space.

Martha Schwartz faced this problem when she was commissioned to create a garden in the atrium, only two and a half storeys high, of the Becton Dickinson Immunocytometry Division medical research building in San Jose, California. The narrow, glass-roofed space is no more than a very long hallway, linking offices and leading to the cafeteria.

Schwartz's solution for the scheme, which was completed in 1990, was to divide this featureless space into a series of twelve garden rooms defined by

instant "hedges." These are in fact crate-like wooden boxes made from rows of horizontal timbers, equally spaced and planted with ficus vines that will in time grow to take on the shape of the timber armatures. The height of these "hedges" and the spaces they enclose increase from one end of the hallway to the other. The spaces range from an 8m (36ft) metre square, bordered by a 5m (16½ft) high hedge near the lobby, to a 1.2m (4ft) square space with a hedge only 150mm (6in) high at the far end. The taller, more secluded garden rooms are intended for use for private meetings, while the lower-walled spaces provide seating for the cafeteria.

Each individual "garden room" contains a pool. The blue-tiled edge acts as seating and as a plinth for yellow ball-shaped fountains that spit a single jet of water into the pool. The pool itself contains a raised, red-tiled, circular planter full of sanseveria. Placed along the aisle that runs down the centre of the atrium is a row of fishtail palms with their trunks banded with white horizontal stripes to echo the wooden slats of the partitions. In this scheme Schwartz has achieved an instant transformation of the atrium space by introducing free-standing structures to supplement the planting. In the short term the timber framework defines the space, which will eventually become "greener" as the living elements become established.

INSTITUTE FOR FORESTRY AND NATURE RESEARCH, WAGENINGEN, THE NETHERLANDS

ARCHITECT: **STEFAN BEHNISCH OF BEHNISCH AND PARTNERS**

▲ This plan drawing shows the rectangular experimental planting areas that are arranged across the site. Two of them have glass roofs and are contained within the building itself. The interior gardens are designed to be both decorative and functional.

▶ The industrial-looking building and opening greenhouse-type roof cover a landscape that one would normally expect to find outdoors. The combination of curving paths, low vegetation, and mass planting is widely used in exterior, non-domestic landscape design.

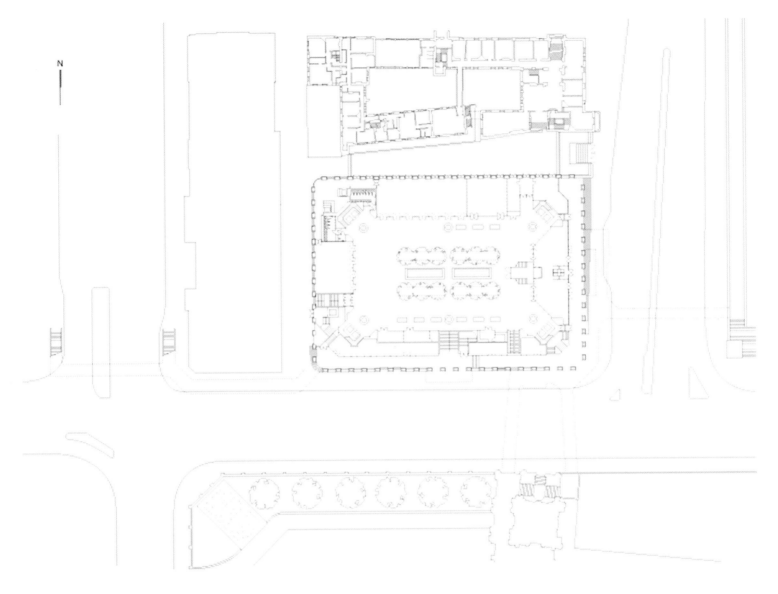

N

ARCHITECTS: **MICHAEL
HOPKINS AND PARTNERS**

◄ An unusual glass roof
protects a spacious, light,
and airy inner courtyard.
The fig trees, which have
room to grow, shade the
cafeteria and sitting areas.

▲ The plan drawing reveals
restrained landscaping
that consists essentially
of four planters arranged
about two central pools.

Another research centre, at Wageningen in the
Netherlands, has not one but two glass-roofed,
internal gardens. At the Institute for Forestry and
Nature Research, designed by the German architect
Stefan Behnisch, of Behnisch, Behnisch and Partners,
each of the rectangular courtyard spaces is flanked on
two sides by three-storey office and laboratory
accommodation. These workplaces are connected at
each of the upper levels by overhanging gangways,
and steel bridges also link the two sides.

Almost the whole of the ground floor is devoted
to a garden that contains a wide variety of shrubs and
herbaceous plants laid out in an informal manner.
Paths zigzag through the planting to connect with

doors and staircases. The informal design and mixed
planting conceal the fact that this is an experimental
garden where plants are being grown under trial
conditions. The glass roof, for instance, is designed to
be functional rather than aesthetically pleasing – it
is a modern greenhouse roof with automatic
mechanisms that open and close vents to keep the
greenhouse at the required temperature.

Today, the main function of a glass-roofed garden
or winter garden is as a leisure facility in the
workplace rather than a place in which to grow or
study plants. In the planning of major architectural
schemes, both public and private, a covered interior
garden space is often requested by clients.

The German architects Hentrich, Petschnigg and Partner included an interior garden in their design for a speculative office block in Bonn. Forum Bonn has a high, glazed atrium built over an underground car park. The interior landscape of the atrium was designed by Bodeker, Wagenfeld and Partner and features a central large, rectangular pool that occupies most of the floor space. A modest tiered fountain sits at one end of the pool, while the other end the pool terminates in a spectacular series of curved water steps, which descend in front of a spiral pedestrian staircase that leads down to the car park. For those using the car park, the winter garden serves as the main entrance to the building. The impressive waterfall – the sound of its cascading water audible from the basement – is the feature that links the parking area and the atrium above it.

Planting beds and a pavement flank the pool on both sides, and the pale-grey paving slabs are set within a grid pattern of black stone that echoes the geometry of the steel-and-glass roof. The planting bordering the pool consists of a row equally spaced *Magnolia soulangeana* with ivy as ground cover. Trees set in the planting beds and the pool are illuminated at night by spotlights. The dominance of the pool and the lack of permanent seating suggest that the atrium is a thoroughfare rather than the prized social space of many such interior landscapes.

This is not a criticism that can be levelled at Portcullis House in London, opened in 2001. Designed by Michael Hopkins and Partners, this office building for Members of Parliament and their staff includes a large court covered by a single-span, slightly pointed, barrel-vault glass roof. The lattice of timber and steel that supports the roof covers a recreational interior-exterior space planted with ficus trees and ground cover. The planting is in two pairs of raised containers placed end to end on the long sides of two mirror ponds.

This glazed court encapsulates the benefit of gardens under glass. In countries such as Britain the weather, even in summer, often prevents the use of exterior gardens as places for social or private leisure activities. The reinvention of the winter garden has seen the return of the weatherproof garden.

SEA HAWK HOTEL AND RESORT, FUKUOKA, JAPAN
ARCHITECTS: **BALMORI ASSOCIATES AND CESAR PELLI ASSOCIATES**

LANDSCAPE **ARCHITECTS: SOMA LANDSCAPE PLANNING CO., LTD**

▶ This vast steel-and-glass barrel roof looks like it belongs to the nineteenth century, although it was actually built at the end of the twentieth. Beneath its canopy a cafe occupies a clearing within a dense jungle of large foliage plants, towering palms, and eucalyptus.

index ▶ ▶ ▶ ▶ ▶

Page numbers in italics refer to illustrations

photographic acknowledgments

Mitchell Beazley would like to thank all those who have so kindly provided images for use in this book. All plans and drawings have been supplied by the architects or designers credited in captions. Photographic acknowledgements are as follows.

Key: a above, **b** below, **l** left, **r** right

1 Parc de la Villette/Pascal Dolémieux; **2** Charles Mann Photography Inc; **4–5** Danadjieva & Koenig Associates/J F Housel; **8** Galen R Frysinger; **9** Giraudon/Bridgeman Art Library; **10** AKG London/Thomas Gade; **11a** National Trust Photographic Library/Derek Harris; **11b** Mary Evans Picture Library; **12a** Impact/Mark Henley; **12b** Axiom/Jim Holmes; **13** Japan Architect Co/Shinkenchiku-Sha; **16, 17** Isamu Noguchi Foundation Inc/Michio Noguchi; **18** Japan Architect Co/Shinkenchiku-Sha; **20** Shunmyo Masuko/Haruo Hirota; **22a** & **b**, **23** Household; **24** Nikken Sekkei Ltd/Shinkenchiku-Sha; **26, 27** Arcaid/John Edward Linden; **29** Xaveer de Geyter Architecten BVBA; **31, 32** Ron Herman Landscape Architect Inc (www.rherman.com)/Ron Herman and Mark Schwartz; **34** Shigeru Ban/Hiroyuki Hirai; **36** Harpur Garden Library/Jerry Harpur; **37** Claire de Virieu; **38** Kisho Kurohawa Architect & Associates; **39** Parc de la Villette/Arnaud Legrain; **42, 43, 44, 45** T R Hamzah & Yeang Sdn Bhd; **46,48** Log ID; **51** Herzog & Partner; **52, 54** Log ID; **55** Bill Dunster Architects; **56l** & **r** Peter Beck/Böro für Stadtökologie; **58** Log ID; **61** Kida Katsuhisa; **62** Shigeru Ban/Hiroyuki Hirai; **64** Emilio Ambasz & Associates, Inc; **68** Dani Karavan/Werner J Hannapel; **70** ©2001 Joram Harel, Vienna, H Kluger; **71a** & **b** Barbara Gladstone; **72** Arcaid/John Edward Linden; **73** Nicola Browne; **74** Balmori Associates; **76, 77** Esto/Peter Aaron; **78, 79** Dominique Kippelen/Jean-Baptiste Dorner; **80** Latz & Partner/Christa Panick; **82, 83** Tim Street-Porter; **84–5** ©2001 Joram Harel, Vienna /H Kluger; **86–87, 88, 89** Arcaid/Alan Weintraub; **90** Tadao Ando Architect & Associates; **91** Martha Schwartz Inc/Peter Walker; **94–5** Arcaid/Ian Lambot; **96** Studio On Site; **98, 99** Norman McGrath; **100** John Portman & Associates/Tim Hursley; **103a** & **b** Kevin Roche John Dinkeloo & Associates; **104** Peddle Thorp Architects/Bruce Peebles; **106** TVS/Brian Gassel; **107** WET Design/Ira Kahn; **108,109** Danadjieva & Koenig Associates/ J F Housel; **111** Architecture Studio/Gaston; **112** Gardens Illustrated/Le Scanff-Mayer; **116, 118** Shigeru Ban/Hiroyuki Hirai; **120** Waro Kishi & K Associates/Hiroyuki Hirai; **122** Souto Moura Arquitectos Lda/Luís Ferreirra Alves; **124** Charles Correa/Claire Arni; **127** Arcaid/John Edward Linden; **128** Malcolm Birkitt; **130** Arcaid/Richard Bryant; **132** Derek St Romaine; **133** Bernard St-Denis; **134** Nicola Browne; **135** Charles Mann Photography Inc; **136** Timothy Hursley; **139** Legorreta & Legorreta/Loudes Legorreta; **140-1** Bochsler & Partners; **142-3** Archer Mortlock & Woolley Pty Ltd/Eric Sierins; **144** Studio On Site; **148, 149** Wildlife Matters; **150** VIEW/Peter MacKinwen; **152-3** VIEW/Peter Cook; **154, 155** Trevor Mein; **156** SITE; **158, 159** Creative Sources Photography Inc/Rion Rizzo; **160, 162, 163** Georg Penkr; **164, 165** Werner Huthmacher; **166, 167** Martha Schwartz Inc/David Meyer; **169** Peter Blundell Jones; **170** Michael Hopkins & Partners; **172-3** Balmori Associates.